Above: Citrus fruit studded with cloves and arranged with natural greens, Joseph Manigault House, Charleston
Overleaf: Meeting House in winter, Table Rock State Park

A South Carolina Christmas

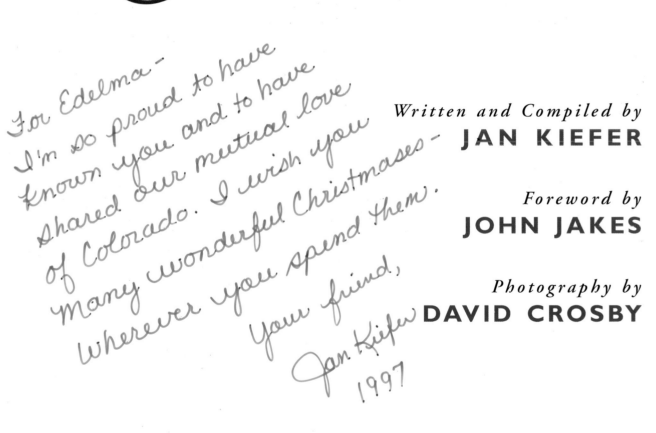

For Edelma –
I'm so proud to have
known you and to have
shared our mutual love
of Colorado. I wish you
many wonderful Christmases –
wherever you spend them.
Your friend,
Jan Kiefer
1997

Written and Compiled by
JAN KIEFER

Foreword by
JOHN JAKES

Photography by
DAVID CROSBY

WESTCLIFFE PUBLISHERS

ENGLEWOOD, COLORADO

I WOULD LIKE TO EXPRESS SPECIAL THANKS TO:
My mother, Charlotte, who at the age of 80 spent many hours
at the computer keystroking portions of this book, and who also helped
taste test a number of the recipes; Alleene Petty Kracht, Ann Keeter,
and Rhett and Betty Jackson of The Happy Bookseller in Columbia,
who so capably ran the South Carolina Taste Test.

—J.K.

EDITOR: Suzanne Venino
DESIGNER: Rebecca Finkel, F + P Graphic Design
PRODUCTION MANAGER: Harlene Finn,
Westcliffe Publishers

TEXT
© 1997 Jan Kiefer. ALL RIGHTS RESERVED.

FOREWORD
© 1997 John Jakes. ALL RIGHTS RESERVED.

PHOTOGRAPHY
© 1997 David Crosby. ALL RIGHTS RESERVED.

INTERNATIONAL STANDARD BOOK NUMBER
1-56579-237-8

PUBLISHER'S CATALOGING-IN-PUBLICATION
Kiefer, Jan.
   A South Carolina Christmas /
written and compiled by Jan Kiefer ;
foreword by John Jakes ; photography
by David Crosby.   – 1st ed.

   p. cm.
   Includes index.
   ISBN 1-56579-237-8

   1. Christmas—South Carolina.
2. South Carolina—Social life and
customs. I. Title.

GT4986,S6K54 1997   394.2663'09757
                  QBI97-40694

PUBLISHER
Westcliffe Publishers, Inc.
2650 South Zuni Street
Englewood, Colorado 80110

PRINTED IN HONG KONG BY
WORLD PRINT LTD

For information about other fine books and
calendars from Westcliffe Publishers, please contact
your local bookstore or contact us by calling
(303) 935-0900, faxing (303) 935-0903,
or writing us for a free catalogue.

TABLE OF CONTENTS

Camillias at Hopsewee Plantation

Quick Reference

FOREWORD

When I was a boy growing up on the winter-bound streets of Chicago (yes, I confess it: the dreaded six-letter word Y————e applies to me), I thought everyone in America shivered from cold and tap-danced on ice going to and from church on Christmas Eve. (In that time and place, we didn't drive half a block to get somewhere, we walked, in this case two blocks to one of the largest Baptist churches in the Midwest.)

Palmettos in early morning, Hunting Island State Park

I thought everyone sat in tense silence on Christmas day as father gripped the steering wheel, white-knuckled, and squinted through the sleet-covered windshield while prayerfully negotiating the snow-drifted streets and black-ice roads leading to Grandma's house.

Twenty years ago, my indentured servitude in the advertising trade ended and I realized I could move my writer's typewriter anywhere I wished. I discovered South Carolina, and all of its warm and genteel people (give or take a few state legislators mired in a mind-set left over from the last century). I also discovered the unique joys my adopted state offers at the Christmas season.

• The loveliness of the Christmas story from St. Luke, read by a native Hilton Head Islander in the flowing, musical syllables of Gullah.

• The delight to be found in a dusting of snow that is almost sure to melt by 11:00 A.M.

• The custom of serving succulent sweet potatoes for the Yuletide meal (a custom new to me), followed by the tasty dish called Hoppin' John for New Year's.

• The pure joy of spending the holiday afternoon in a golf shirt.

These are just a few that come to mind. The actual list of holiday pleasures in South Carolina is much longer, far richer. You will see and read about a great number of them in the colorful pages that follow. You'll find it a grand experience—very nearly as good as enjoying the real thing, as my family and I have for going on twenty years now.

MERRY CHRISTMAS

JOHN JAKES
AUTHOR OF *THE NORTH AND SOUTH* TRILOGY

PREFACE

"Smiling Faces, Beautiful Places," is the tourism motto of South Carolina. I'd heard it and seen it any number of places around the state and had not given it too much thought, except to briefly consider that somebody probably won an advertising award for dreaming it up. It sounded like a lot of other tourism slogans to me.

But it couldn't be more true of the people and places of South Carolina. Some of the loveliest smiling faces and certainly some of the most beautiful places in the country are indeed right here in South Carolina. As I criss-crossed the state, talking with the people about their Christmas celebrations, faces lit up with smiles, and I began to recognize how utterly proud people are to be South Carolinians.

It is a place of great diversity: from restored colonial splendor to modern international technology; from the simplicity of shrimp fishermen to the graciousness of elegant city dwellers; from renowned intellectuals at noted universities to old-time storytellers still living in mountain hollows. No matter what walk of life they claim, the people of South Carolina always have a ready smile and no end to helpfulness.

South Carolina has figured more prominently than most other states in American history books. Since its early days as a royal British colony, through the Revolutionary War and the Civil War, when its economy was completely devastated, the state of South Carolina has stood proud and strong. Generations of families working together have rebuilt it to the great state it is today. Roots are deep here and a sense of history abounds.

South Carolina is a wonderful place to be at any time of the year, but especially at Christmas when the state is all dressed up in holiday splendor. There may not be much snow, but there is an abundance of Christmas spirit. Most South Carolinians will tell you that it's what's inside that counts, and they prove it over and over in their kindness and generosity—in the gifts of their smiling faces and beautiful places.

Jan E. Kuifu

Right: Beaufort Bay
Overleaf: Grist mill, Oconee County

Dedicated with love to my guardians, Mel and Jane Kellar,
who, with their children, became my family at Christmas
for six of my teenage years.

—J.K.

CHRISTMAS PAST
A HISTORIC PERSPECTIVE
by C. Patton Hash, South Carolina State Historian

Christmas in Charleston was almost forgotten in 1892. Certainly the stores were filled with candy and gifts, and King Street was packed with shoppers. Decorations were all about and Santa Claus was to make his rounds. But a great threat loomed over the city, indeed, over the entire Lowcountry. Governor "Pitchfork" Ben Tillman was pushing to pass the Dispensary Act, limiting liquor sales to state-controlled businesses. And as the cruelest blow, he was to have it voted on, of all days, Christmas Eve.

The city newspapers were outraged. *The News and Courier* referred to "the incapacity and blundering zeal which prompted and promoted the passage of this extraordinary measure of legislation." The editorial bluster that was normally reserved for great crises of policy was unleashed on this nefarious act. Reading the editorials, one would think the dispensary system was the most vile threat that Carolinians had faced since Sherman's March in 1865. And on a day marked by whiskeyed mince pies, brandy-soaked plum puddings, and rum-laden eggnog! South Carolinians would not surrender their Christmas traditions! The dreaded bill passed, but was eventually overturned.

The celebration of Christmas is very much a part of the treasured memory of South Carolina. In addition to Christmas trees and plenteous gifts, there are oyster roasts, firecrackers, bottles of Madeira, and grand entertainment. South Carolinians have always celebrated the season with enthusiasm, adapting our own unique traditions to the day.

Charleston was settled after the restoration of Charles II to the English throne. His predecessor, Oliver Cromwell, and his henchmen, the Roundheads, were a rather dull sort and looked disparagingly upon Christmas, what with its boisterous drinking, carousing, and caroling. Cromwell banned all observances of the day and arrested those who celebrated. When Charles and the Stuarts returned, Christmas was restored, but it was now celebrated in a much more modest and less clamorous fashion.

In its first century, Charleston seems to have celebrated Christmas in this English way. We don't know much about specific customs, because the first settlers left little mention of the feast. However, an article in the *South Carolina Gazette* of December 14, 1734 offers a clue to how the early Carolinians celebrated. The writer, using the pen name of Gallio, divided the populace into four groups: "1. That some Christians celebrate this Season in a mixture of Piety and Licentiousness. 2. Others perform their Offices in a pious way only. 3. Many behave themselves profusely and extravagantly alone. And 4. Too many, who call themselves Christians, pass over this holy Time, without paying any regard to it at all."

Annual candlelight carriage tours, Fountain Inn

Smoke house in ice storm, Mountain Rest

Walnut Grove Plantation, near Spartanburg

When Sherman's troops came through Fairfield County, my family was ready for them. The livestock had been hidden deep in the woods, hams were stashed away under the stair landing, and my great, great, great aunt suspended the family silver underneath her big hoop skirt. The livestock, hams, and silver remained safe when the soldiers came. One of the soldiers picked up great, great aunt's doll. She went running up to him, yelling, "Please don't take my doll!" He placed the doll on the fence post as he rode out of the yard.

—JUDY C. MILLINAX
formerly of Jenkinsville

Henry Laurens, a wealthy Charleston merchant, wrote of his Christmas in 1763, saying he was "just going to make half a holyday at Rattray Green [a subsection of present-day Ansonboro in Charleston] in quiet while the whole Town almost seems to be using every means in their power to testify that they are true Christians."

One thing that is certain is that many early South Carolinians "profusely and extravagantly" enjoyed the fruit of the vine during the season. A writer to the *Gazette* on December 24, 1772 expressed great concern about individuals partaking of the "exhilarating Cup" which "dissipates their Cares," warning "that Ebriety and Lewdness carry with them their own certain and severe Punishment."

During the Christmas season, newspapers were filled with numerous advertisements for rum, brandy, claret, beer, ale, baskets of champagne, and, most often, the drink of choice of our ancestors—Madeira. Different from other wines because its taste improves with the heat, Madeira was peculiarly adapted for the South, and Carolinians quaffed it with elan. While presiding over the Continental Congress and confined to bed with gout for sixteen days, Henry Laurens wrote, "I have drank 16 bottles less Madeira than I should have otherwise done & consequently have 16 times…more to spare for Christmas Boxes." A Carolina table was never complete without a few bottles of "superior old Madeira," which were as treasured as heirloom silver.

Perhaps the most distinctive part of the holiday throughout the South and South Carolina is the cracking of fireworks after the stockings have been emptied on Christmas morning. Other regions have quiet, snow-filled Yule holidays, but not the South, where it wouldn't be Christmas without a full-scale re-enactment of the artillery barrage at Fredericksburg on some nearby snowless slope. A few historians have theorized that this custom comes from the French in Louisiana, but that it is not true to South Carolina. It was the practice of mummers in pre-Restoration England to go about town banging drums, blowing horns, and shooting guns to celebrate the season. Since nearly every man in South Carolina owned a gun, and many boys would receive their first guns at Christmas, it seems logical that they would use Christmas Day to try out their firearms and carry on this tradition.

By the late-18th century, when cheap fireworks became available, there were, not surprisingly, numerous injuries noted in the newspapers, from both fireworks and guns. A *Charleston Times* news-carrier enjoying his "Christmas gamboll" was severely injured in 1801 "from the blowing up of some powder…so as to prevent him from attending to his duty." It became such a nuisance that by 1806 the city marshal ran a notice in the *Times* of city ordinances that outlawed "the idle and dangerous practice of Beating Drums,

Firing Guns & within the city" at Christmas as well as the rest of the year. Such laws were apparently difficult to enforce and eventually certain areas were set aside within the city for "legal" explosions. These included Gadsden Green, White Point Gardens, Hampstead Mall, and the west end of Broad Street.

Many young people, primarily the children of the wealthy, had no reason to be concerned about city ordinances because they were not in town during the holiday season. Most plantation owners and their families were in the country in December. It was the time to complete the harvest and mill the rice, the time to pick long-staple cotton, and also the time to issue clothes to the slaves for the upcoming year. Joseph Manigault, writing from Charleston in late December 1786 to his brother Gabriel in Goose Creek, said it was "unfashionable to be here at this season.... You meet nobody but Shopkeepers and Tradesmen, I am heartily tired of their vulgar countenances...."

A plantation Christmas was the result of long hours of work on the part of the mistress and the house servants. In a scene typical of the time, Sally Baxter Hampton, sister-in-law of Wade Hampton III, described preparations at Woodlands plantation in Richland County in 1860. She was at work, she wrote, "in the store room, in the pantry, presiding over first the boiling of hops and making of yeast for the necessary Xmas loaves, & after wards the selection of fat poultry, the cutting of a saddle of mutton, the proper picking of game, the making & baking of cakes & confections ordinary & extraordinary...these are all the necessary duties of a Southern housekeeper."

Colonel John Ashe House,
on the Battery, Charleston

Feverish work to complete the harvest and preparations for the holiday continued until Christmas Day, when all work stopped for three to six days. This made Christmas the day of days to slaves. In his book *Down By the Riverside,* Charles Joyner describes the day as beginning with house servants running through the house yelling "Christmas gift" and "I got you," at which the gotten (the master's family) would have to produce a gift for the "getter" (the slave). Later that morning extra rations were issued to the hands on the plantation, an ox would be slaughtered, perhaps a few hogs, and a barbecue would commence.

Christmas was also one of the few times when slaves were given whiskey, often from the front steps of the house. Mrs. R. F. W. Allston wrote her son that on Christmas morning 1856 the slaves toasted Mr. Allston's election as governor on the front piazza of Chicora Wood with "many a stout glass of whiskey."

In our family it has always been a tradition to greet late arrivals at the family gathering on Christmas morning with the greeting "Chrismus gif!" which is called out loudly and with great fervor. If the one greeted protests, the greeter responds with "I gotcha, I gotcha!" This means that the one who was "got" now owes the greeter a special Christmas present. This routine continues until everyone has arrived and been greeted with "Chrismus gif!" Of course, the more persons one can "get," the more special presents one can anticipate. Our family still holds to this old custom and makes much of deciding who owes what to whom.

—EULA MAY CARLISLE STOCKMAN, *Greenville*

The first running of "The Best Friend of Charleston" occurred in 1830 on Christmas Day. The train ran from the Line Street depot to a point six miles from the city. The passengers "flew on the wings of the wind at the speed of fifteen to twenty-five miles per hour, annihilating time and space and leaving all the world behind," as one passenger recorded.

—C. PATTON HASH
Charleston

Live oaks, Rochelle Plantation, Georgetown

*Dancing the quadrille,
Robert Mills House,
Columbia*

*When I was a little girl, the children
always put on a play at church on
Christmas Eve. After the pageant, we
would sing carols, and at the end of
the service everyone was given a
brown paper bag filled with apples,
oranges, raisins on stems, a few nuts,
and one big stick of peppermint candy.*

— DOT THOMPSON
Greenville

This "off time" was also a season for slave weddings. Mrs. William Bull Pringle described an 1856 Christmas Eve communion service and marriage, performed by the Reverend John Drayton-Grimke in the Magnolia Plantation chapel. "For Mr. Drayton's usual service to the Blacks, first, we had service, then Communion, to whites and blacks, and, then we had the marriage ceremony." Their servant Penny was married to a slave of Mr. Ramsey's. The bride "appeared in a neat white dress and plain handkerchief…and they had a wedding ring, with all the paraphernalia of a veritable marriage ceremony." Usually a dance would follow. It was not uncommon for there to be several dances in the quarters during Christmastime.

The great event of Christmas on the plantation was the dinner, when all the bounty of the land was placed on a groaning table. Perhaps the most evocative description of a Yuletide feast is found in *Rumbling of the Chariot Wheels,* written by I. Jenkins Mikell and published in 1923. He gives no date in his account, but one can assume that it comes from 1860 or earlier. The invitation came from the owner of Bleak Hall on Edisto Island with the following words: "We hope to see you and yours at Bleak Hall on the 27th to join us in our Christmas festivities—an oyster roast."

Twenty-five friends and neighbors were invited, and the meal was held under the great oaks. Fires were lit at noon, and the oysters were poured on the coals when the guests arrived at one. Each place at the table was set with a "Plate mat of coarse linen to hold the wooden platters of oysters, an oyster cloth on the left, an oyster knife…on the right. A tumbler for each was not left off. First came the butler with a silver pitcher of steaming hot punch, filling the glasses; hot, old time, knock down drag out whiskey punch, not your Manhattan or Bronx poison, but punch made of lemons, hot water, sugar, and double-proof imported Irish peat whiskey."

The host toasted his guests and then the sizzling oysters were placed on the platters. "For a time nothing was heard save the knife struggling with an obdurate oyster." Then came a rest, a stroll, and then a return to fully set tables. Mikell continues, "A Description would be beyond my power…Lucullus [of ancient Rome] 'had nothing on it' in the way of a feast…. [And] we had what I know he did not have—palmetto cabbage. The name 'cabbage' is a misnomer and unfortunate. It is no more like that popular and plebeian

dish than a capon is like a crow…. It has the combined taste of a cauliflower, burr artichoke, and asparagus, with the most fascinating and predominant taste of its own…. Lucullus doubtless had an orchestra, ours was the sighing of wind through the moss-bearded oaks; the ceaseless chatter of palmetto fronds, the soft deep booming of the surf one hundred yards away, interspersed with the high staccato pop of a champagned cork." This was the ultimate Lowcountry Christmas feast!

*Jenny Lind, Charleston, 1850
(From the collections of the South Carolina Historical Society)*

If one were in Charleston during the Christmas season, there was usually no lack of entertainment. Circuses made the city a regular stop during December, as did acting troupes. The most famous Yuletide entertainment was the "Swedish Nightingale," Jenny Lind. The excitement rose to a crescendo pitch with the approach of her visit in 1850, approximating the hysteria we moderns have exhibited toward Frank Sinatra, the Beatles, and Madonna. Anxious bidding played for scarce tickets, and poems and essays to her beauty filled the newspapers. Her promoter was P. T. Barnum and he, of course, did not encourage any of this enthusiasm. She arrived with him on December 23, and they took rooms at the Charleston Hotel. On Christmas Eve the Charleston *Courier* reported, "last evening at her lodgings, a Forest Tree was placed at her window, decorated with variegated lamps, which attracted much attention." This is the first mention that can be found of a Christmas tree in Charleston, or in the state. And while it was likely that earlier German settlers may have had Christmas trees, it was after this that the practice of erecting a tree became common. Soon it seemed that everyone in South Carolina had a tree.

In 1904 the Charleston Hotel continued its role in pioneering Christmas customs, this time with electric lights. After the completion of dinner at six o'clock, the guests at the hotel were invited into the banquet hall. With a twelve-piece orchestra playing in the background, the crowd moved into the room, decorated with boughs of holly and sprigs of mistletoe, palms in jardinieres and flowers in stands. Standing in the center of the room was, "the splendid fir…sparkling with vari-colored electric bulbs, and silver chains and spangles and trinkets, and bells and gift boxes descended from the branches. It was a decided novelty, but everyone was ready for that." Both the *News* and *Courier* noted that because interest in the tree was so great, it was to be illuminated again the night after Christmas.

This covers some of the more secular aspects of Christmas that South Carolinians have enjoyed over the years. Old customs. Family traditions. We cultivate them carefully and protect them assiduously from the hurly-burly of modern times. No matter how simple they are, these traditions become our anchor, landmarks in the ever-increasing swirl of our lives. And it is this essence—as well as the smell of fresh-cut pine, the glow of a tree, or the joy of giving a special gift to a loved one—that is the celebration of the season. This is what Christmas is all about.

It is one of the few times in life when fairy tales do come true and the best in us prevails. We share in a sense of community and giving, of family and faith. Our memories of the day are among our most treasured heirlooms, shining like grandmother's most prized ornament, a brilliant respite in our often restless lives.

"Father, I should be very much obliged to you if you would get me a couple of combs if you please, and a bonnet. I would not ask you if it was not so near Christmas."

—HARRIET AYER
in a letter to her father, Lewis Malone Ayer, November 29, 1806. (From the Ayer Collection, courtesy of the South Caroliniana Library, University of South Carolina.)

"I hope you have passed a Merry Christmas this year. We have passed ours pleasantly…. Instead of a large dinner table surrounded by our relations we had our usual table and the only company was James Cuthbert, who appears to be a very amiable young man, but he is much too silent for us."

—HENRIETTA MANIGAULT
In a letter to her sister, December 26, 1813. (From the Manigault Collection, courtesy of the South Caroliniana Library, University of South Carolina.)

Gullah

A LOWCOUNTRY WAY OF LIFE

If you hear somebody talking about fixin' Hopp'n' John to bring good luck on New Yeah Day, and it sounds a little like a foreign language, it's likely Gullah that you're hearing. Gullah is not a foreign language to the fifteen to twenty thousand folks who still speak it. In fact, Gullah is recognized by linguists as a distinct African-American language, not a dialect, and it is still spoken in the easternmost parts of South Carolina, particularly James Island, Johns Island, Edisto Island, and parts of Charleston and Beaufort.

The Gullah people are descendants of slaves who worked the great South Carolina rice plantations. Their language developed during the days of slavery and endures as part of their culture today. If you listen carefully, Gullah sounds quite a bit like English, and English words do comprise much of the vocabulary, which was acquired from plantation overseers. There are also West African words and the influences of various creole languages spoken by natives of the West Indies. It is a very musical language, with a sing-song lilt.

As with many old languages, the young people tend to look on Gullah as out of date and they prefer to speak English. To help preserve this regional tradition, Dr. Virginia Geraty, professor of Gullah at the College of Charleston, has gone on a mission to help the new generations learn Gullah as a second language. When she is not teaching Gullah, she is at work compiling Gullah dictionaries, and she has also published a Gullah cookbook. Entitled *Bittle 'en t'i'ng,* the cookbook features the recipes of Maum Chrish, who gives the Gullah version, with the English translation provided by Dr. Geraty. Several Christmas and New Year's recipes are included on the following pages.

A Gullah Christmas Day

by Marlena Smalls, Beaufort

(To be read aloud in a sing-song manner)

am a Sea Island descendent. My early childhood was lived through the eyes of my grandmother, Mary Williams Clements, who by all accounts happened to be the world's greatest storyteller.

"Christmastime," Grandma said, "often was high cotton time, no work and play all day. For some it was the celebration of Baby Jesus, but for us slaves, it was freedom or such," Grandma said.

A Gullah Christmas Day was filled with song, dance, and African rhythm that soared to the heavens. One could see a live oak move its branches, wistfully through the music.

Also, it represents a time for unions—that's a marriage, you know, or just simply called "jumping de broom."

Gifts shared were from: nuts to aprons, eggs to baskets, nets to hats, or wooden men to combs.

Now every room was filled with laughter as we prepared to eat Grandma's favorite dishes: turkey, red rice, collard greens—you know, seasoned with just a little fat back—and field peas that would make you shake hands with the devil, just to taste a bite.

And we gained a pound or two, just from the sight of sweet 'tater poon, bread pudding, black berry cobbler, and many others.

Now, when dinner was done and sharing time continued, we'd glance around the room to view the pine needles, cones, red ribbons, popcorn, and berry crowns that claimed the room on Christmas Day.

Grandma said, "I could still hear old Reverend John Milton belt out "O Wonder Christmas Star," and the basser joining in with "The angelic choir of heaven soon to follow."

Actress and singer Marlena Smalls is founder and director of the Hallelujah Singers. She has dedicated her talent and her knowledge of the Gullah people to preserving many of the traditions of her ancestors, who moved from Africa, through slavery, and finally into freedom on South Carolina's shores and islands.

Jumping de Broom

Well, if it is your desire to wed,
and it's Christmas Day you said,

Remember…jump high, jump high,
touch the sky;

For if you touch this broom

You'll be the first to die.

HOPP'N' JOHN

If you work on New Year's Day and eat Hopping John for dinner, you will be healthy and able to work every day of the year.

Be sure to soak the peas on New Year's Eve, because that is the time the peas "take up" the luck.

The next morning take:
  1 cup dried field peas
  1 medium onion, chopped
  1 cup cooked smoked pork, chopped
  4 cups water
  1 cup rice
  1 teaspoon salt

Boil the peas with the onion and the meat until the peas are nearly done. Drain the peas, but save the water they were cooked in.

In another pot, put the rice and the peas with the meat and onion. Add three cups of water from the peas. Add the salt and cook until the rice is done.

This will feed a large family and keep them healthy all year.

HOPP'N' JOHN

Mus' sho' en' wu'k New Yeah Day, en' mus' sho' en' nyam Hopp'n' John. Hopp'n' John fetch de luck fuh oonuh able fuh wu'k eb'ry day ub de New Yeah.

Mus' don' fuhgit fuh soak de fiel' pea on New Yeah Ebe, so de pea hab chance fuh tek up de good luck wuh come fu'm middlenight tuh dayclean.

W'en 'e dayclean New Yeah mawn'n', tek:

1 medjuh ub fiel' pea	1 medjum onyun (chop up)
4 medjuh ub watuh	1 leetle spoon ub salt
1 medjuh ub rice	
1 medjuh ub cook smoke side (chop up)	

Bile de pea, de meat, 'en de onyun een de watuh 'tell de pea mos' done. Sabe de pot-likkuh.

Pit de pea en' de meat en' de onyun een uh nex' pot 'long de rice en' pit t'ree medjuh ub pot-likkuh 'cross 'um. T'row de salt 'cross 'um en' cook 'um 'tell de rice grain suffuhrate.

Dis 'nuf fuh de fambly, en' dem gwi' hop libely eb'ry day de hole yeah long.

SILLYBUB

Take :
    4 cups of cream
    1 cup of milk
    1 cup of white wine
    2 tablespoons sugar

Beat them together until it looks like the foam that comes off the ocean waves.

Grandma used to take the bowl to the cow and milk her directly into the bowl to get the foam. Maum doesn't trust Bossy not to switch her tail in the milk.

Pour it into twelve sherbet glasses.

SILLYBUB (SYLLABUB)

Tek:

4 medjuh ub cow cream	1 medjuh ub wine
1 medjuh ub cow milk	2 laa'ge spoon ub suguh

Lick 'um tuhgedduh 'tell 'e stan' samelukkuh de foam wuh come off de wabe top down tuh de salt.

Gramma nyusetuh cya' de bowl tuh de cow en' milk 'um fuh 'e foam. Uh yent trus' fuh do dat; Bossy too lub fuh swish 'e tail!

Po 'um een twelbe leetle glass.

*All recipes reprinted with permission from **Bittle 'en t'i'ng** by Virginia Geraty, Lh.D., Sandlapper Publishing, Inc.*

SWEET 'TETTUH PIE
(SWEET POTATO PIE)

Bile t'ree mejum sweet 'tettuh 'tell dem done. Mus' don' peel de 'tettuh 'tell dey done bile. Den peel'um en' mash'um 'long one medjuh ub suguh.

Lick-up uh aig, en' mix'um wid one medjuh ub milk. Mix de aig en de milk wid de 'tettuh en' de suguh.

Seaz'n 'um wid:

½ leetle spoor ub cinmamun   3 laa'gee spoon ub melt buttuh

¼ leetle spoon ub natt'n'aig   ¼ leetle spoon ub salt

2 laa'ge spoon ub banilluh

Po' dis mixjuh een uh raw crus' en' bake'um een uh medjum hot obun 'tell 'e settle down en' tu'n browng.

SWEET POTATO PIE
Preheat oven to 350° F.

Boil three medium-size sweet potatoes in their skins till done. Peel them and mash them with one cup of sugar.

Beat one egg and mix it with one cup of milk. Mix the egg and milk with the potato and sugar.

Season the mixture with:
    ½ teaspoon of cinnamon
    ¼ teaspoon of nutmeg
    2 tablespoons of vanilla
    3 tablespoons of melted butter
    ¼ teaspoon of salt

Put the mixture into an unbaked pie shell and bake it in a medium hot oven until the filling is set and turns brown.

Highly prized for their superior craftsmanship, Gullah sweetgrass baskets are a favorite Christmas gift in South Carolina. Along the streets of historic Charleston and in its famed Old City Market, Gullah women weave these beautiful baskets in the traditional manner passed on through many generations.

Above: Brick Baptist Church, where Saint Helena Hymn was first sung on Christmas Day in 1862

Below: Ruins of an old church built of tabby, a cement made from crushed oyster shell, sand, and lime, St. Helena Island

SAINT HELENA HYMN

The Saint Helena Hymn was written by John Greenleaf Whittier in 1862. Charlotte Forten, the first Black from the North to come to St. Helena to teach, requested him to write the song for the people of the island.

Oh, none in all the world before
Were ever glad as we,
We're free on Carolina's shore
We're all at home and free.

Thou friend and helper of the poor
Who suffered for our sake,
To open every prison door
And every yoke to break.

Bend low they pitying face and mild
And help us sing and pray,
The hand that blessed the little child
Upon our foreheads lay.

We hear no more the driver's horn,
No more the whip we fear
This holy day that saw thee born,
Was never half so dear.

The very oaks are greener clad
The waters brighter smile,
Oh, never shown a day so glad
On sweet St. Helena's Isle.

We praise thee in our songs today
To thee in prayer we call,
Make swift the feet and straight the way
Of freedom unto all.

Come once again, O blessed Lord
Come walking on the sea,
And let the mainlands hear the word
That sets the Island free.

*From the Penn School Collection.
Reprinted with permission by Penn Center, Inc.,
St. Helena Island, South Carolina*

Right: Historic Brattonsville Plantation, near Rock Hill

Below: Colonial Christmas re-enactment at Brattonsville

Christmas Twice in Historic Brattonsville

Candles made of tallow once lit the home of Colonel Bratton, an officer in the Revolutionary Army. Today volunteers in period dress bring history to life as they guide holiday visitors through the historic homestead on a candlelight tour. The restored farmhouse, outbuildings, and grounds are decorated for the season as more than 80 volunteers reenact what life was once like in rural South Carolina. This award-winning living history program is unique in that it portrays two different periods—Christmas in 1780 and in 1850. Through these dramatic presentations, it is easy to imagine that you have stepped back in time.

Drayton Hall

ANNUAL SPIRITUALS CONCERT

For more than 250 years, stately Drayton Hall has remained essentially intact, the only Ashley River plantation house to survive the ravages of Union troops advancing through South Carolina. The Georgian-Palladian architecture, symmetrical and orderly with bold detail, was quite sophisticated when the house was built in the mid-1700s. Its two-story portico is believed to be the first of its kind in America. A variety of free and enslaved craftsmen, including Europeans and Africans, spent four years constructing the mansion, with native and imported materials. Today, this historic building hosts a number of events, and at Christmastime the Great Hall comes alive with the sound of African-American spirituals.

Each year in mid-December, the Annual Spirituals Concert brings to life a musical tradition as old as the mansion itself—music that reflects the faith and hope, the tears and the fears of generations of Africans brought to America as slaves. There are work songs, love songs, and songs of toil and struggle, most all dating back to the days of slavery. Thinking about the coming of Christ was a time of great hope for slaves who longed for freedom. The singers perform these inspirational spirituals a cappella, accompanied only by traditional rhythmic double-clapping. There are no electric lights in Drayton Hall, so the audience is bathed in the soft glow of candlelight, the enduring spirit of the season, and the soulful songs of days long past.

Above: The Senior Lights of Johns Island performing at Drayton Hall
Overleaf: Drayton Hall Plantation, on the Ashley River, near Charleston

Hobcaw Barony

GEORGETOWN

As was the custom on Southern plantations, Christmas was a time of celebration and feasting, for the slaves as well as the landowners. Hobcaw Barony near Georgetown has seen many Christmas celebrations over the centuries. Created as a barony by King

George I in 1718, it was later divided into a number of smaller tracts, many of which became prosperous rice plantations.

In this century it became the winter home of Bernard Baruch, who in 1903 began purchasing the various pieces of property, and nearly completely reassembled the original barony. Baruch, a politician and statesman, counted Winston Churchill among his many friends, and it is said that Churchill wrote a portion of his memoirs while staying at the estate. The home burned down in 1929, and in 1937 Baruch's daughter, Belle, built her own home here, on the estate she called Bellefield Plantation.

Early snow drops bloom at Friendfield Village, former slave quarters at Hobcaw Barony

Belle was known for her lavish New Year's Day luncheons, and judging from her guest registers, she entertained members of some of the most prestigious families in North and South Carolina, as well as her father's famous political friends. She died in 1964, leaving Hobcaw Barony to The Belle W. Baruch Foundation, which is dedicated to researching and teaching in the fields of forestry and marine biology as well as to the care and propagation of flora and fauna native to South Carolina.

Belle's long-time friend, Ella A. Severin, a foundation trustee, resides at Bellefield Plantation, and to this day, even though she is well into her 90's, Miss Severin still holds the traditional New Year's Luncheon. The 1996 party was especially grand. Every corner of the estate was decorated with natural greens; garlands were hung on all the fireplaces and even on the antique carriages brought out of the stables for the occasion. Belle Baruch's childhood angel topped the magnificent Christmas tree, and her nativity scene adorned the harpsichord. There were decorated gingerbread houses, and, of course, food was abundant, including Miss Severin's own plum pudding. Miss Severin plans to hold the New Year's luncheon as long as she is able, continuing the grand tradition of holiday parties at Hobcaw Barony.

MERRY CHRISTMAS COOKIES

3½ cups nuts, pecans or walnuts

1 cup candied cherries

1 cup dates

¾ cup white raisins

3 slices candied pineapple

½ cup butter, softened

½ cup brown sugar

2 eggs, well beaten

1 cups all-purpose flour

½ teaspoon baking soda

½ teaspoon cinnamon

¼ cup milk

1 tablespoon sherry flavoring

Preheat oven to 300° F.

Chop fruit and nuts, and set aside. In a large bowl, cream butter and sugar; add eggs and mix well. In a separate bowl, sift together flour, baking soda and cinnamon. Alternately add the dry ingredients and the milk to the creamed sugar mixture. Add flavoring, fruit and nuts, and mix well.

Drop teaspoon-size dough onto well-greased cookie sheet. Bake for 20 minutes.

Makes about 5 dozen cookies

—**JUDITH W. ERICKSON,** *Greenville*

SUGAR COOKIES

½ cup butter (1 stick)

½ cup margarine (1 stick)

½ cup granulated sugar

¼ cup light brown sugar

¾ teaspoon baking powder

1 egg

1 teaspoon vanilla

2 cups all-purpose flour

½ cup ground nuts, any kind you prefer

Glaze

2 cup confectioners' sugar

2 tablespoons heavy cream

To make cookie dough, cream butter, margarine, sugars, and baking powder in a large bowl. Add egg and vanilla, and mix well. In a separate bowl, combine flour and nuts, and add to creamed mixture, mixing well. Chill.

Preheat oven to 375° F. Roll out dough and cut into shapes using holiday cookie cutters. Bake about 12 minutes until edges are lightly brown. Cool.

To make glaze, combine sugar and cream, and microwave on high for a total of 30 seconds, stirring till blended at 15 second intervals.

Dip cookies in glaze and set on rack to dry. Sprinkle with colored sugar while still wet.

Makes about 3 dozen medium cookies

—**JOHN RUTLEDGE HOUSE INN,** *Charleston*

Our favorite family tradition takes place at Thanksgiving. After church on Wednesday, my children and I travel from Greenville to Pickens to spend the weekend with my parents. On Thanksgiving morning the "girls in the family"— myself, three daughters, my mother, two aunts, and a cousin—gather at the home of one of the aunts and spend the day baking Christmas cookies. We make about 25 dozen, enough to fill two large containers for each family to use during the holidays. We have the same cookie-making duties every year. Several of us chop the fruit and nuts and measure the ingredients, one aunt mixes the dough, and another aunt is in charge of baking. My mother packs the cookies in containers and also makes trips to her house to check on the turkey. The whole family then gathers for a traditional Thanksgiving dinner at my mother's house, where the turkey has been cooking all day. On Friday morning the "girls" gather to go shopping. We sing Christmas carols on the way. None of us can really sing, but nobody cares and we all join in. We spend the entire day Christmas shopping and then go back to my mother's house for leftovers.

—**JUDITH W. ERICKSON**
Greenville

Holiday sweets at the John Rutledge House Inn, Charleston

A Tale of Two Friends
by Ramona Woo, Greenville

My friend Doris Reaser and I have been baking Christmas goodies together for nearly 25 years. Even though Doris has lived in other parts of the state, this tradition has survived—because "it wouldn't be Christmas" if we didn't get together. So we always put everything aside and take turns traveling cross-state for our "baking weekend."

The early years were filled with trial and error. We even had to discard some pots and pans. I think we have now perfected our art to the point that we could even be friends of Martha's (Stewart, that is). We have had so much fun shopping for ingredients. Dates or raisins? Cups or pounds? Chopped or ground? Are you *sure?* And even though we have seen a decline in consumption of sugar and fat grams, most of our friends and neighbors continue to look forward to receiving our homemade goodies. In fact, a lot of friends stop by during our baking weekend to visit and sample.

The first couple of years we made only one batch of each sweet, but as our families have grown we now triple each recipe—and sometimes even that is not enough! Our standard fare is peanut butter balls, chocolate-covered cherries, yule logs, pecan logs, nut fingers, turtles, melt-aways, white and dark chocolate-coated toasted pecans, and Merry Christmas cookies (seven cups of pecans in this recipe!). Everybody's favorite is our peanut butter balls.

PEANUT BUTTER BALLS

1 cup (2 sticks) butter or margarine
1 1-pound box confectioners' sugar
1 cup graham cracker crumbs
½ cup chunky-style peanut butter
1 cup finely ground pecans
1 teaspoon vanilla
1 4-ounce bar household paraffin
2 12-ounce packages semi-sweet chocolate

Melt butter or margarine in a large sauce pan. Stir in confectioners' sugar until smooth. Add cracker crumbs, peanut butter, pecans, and vanilla, and mix well. Shape into 1-inch balls and set aside on waxed paper.

Melt paraffin in double boiler according to package directions. Add chocolate and stir until chocolate is melted and well blended with the paraffin. Dip peanut butter balls into chocolate mixture and set on waxed paper to dry.

Makes about 72 peanut butter balls.

—RAMONA WOO AND DORIS REASER, *Greenville*

Each Christmas our family makes a large gingerbread house. My husband buys heaps of candy, and then the six of us draw numbers to see what part of the house we'll decorate. Each number represents a side of the house or roof. After it's decorated, the gingerbread house is used as a centerpiece through Christmas Day. Then Christmas evening we eat it.

—MARDI SMITH, *Columbia*

SANDIES

1 cup butter (2 sticks), softened

1 cup margarine (2 sticks), softened

½ cup granulated sugar

¼ cup light brown sugar

4 teaspoons water

2 teaspoons vanilla

2 cups all-purpose flour sifted

2 cups ground nuts, pecans or walnuts

Cream butter, margarine and sugars. Add water and vanilla, and mix well. Combine flour and nuts, and add to creamed mixture. Chill.

Preheat oven to 325° F. Shape dough into balls or desired shapes. Bake for 20 minutes. Cool slightly and roll in confectioners' sugar.

Makes about 6 dozen sandies

—JOHN RUTLEDGE HOUSE INN, *Charleston*

DATE BALLS

½ cup butter (1 stick), softened

1 cup sugar

1 8-ounce package chopped dates

1 egg, beaten

1 teaspoon vanilla

2 cups Rice Krispies

1 cup finely chopped pecans or other nuts

½ cup shredded coconut

Combine butter, sugar, dates, egg and vanilla. Cook over low heat, stirring almost constantly until dates are melted. Add Rice Krispies, nuts and coconut, and mix well.

Measure out a teaspoon of warm dough and roll into 1-inch balls with oiled hands. Balls can be served plain, rolled in confectioners' sugar or dipped in melted chocolate.

Makes 3 – 4 dozen date balls

—JOHN RUTLEDGE HOUSE INN, *Charleston*

CHRISTMAS TOFFEE

½ pound butter (2 sticks)

1 cup sugar

½ cup pecans or almond halves

1 teaspoon vanilla

Put the butter and sugar in a cold, iron skillet. Using a wooden spoon, stir constantly over medium heat until golden brown. Remove from heat and add nuts and vanilla. Pour into a buttered round cake pan and cool. Break into bite-size pieces.

Yields 24 pieces

—ALLEENE KRACHT, *Columbia*

Christmas goodies, John Rutledge House Inn, Charleston

PEANUT BUTTER FUDGE

1 pound brown sugar

1 14-ounce can Carnation condensed milk

12 large marshmallows

1 tablespoon butter

¼ cup peanut butter

1 cup chopped nuts, pecans or walnuts

In a large sauce pan, combine sugar, milk and marshmallows and cook over medium heat to 234° F on a candy thermometer or until a small amount forms a soft ball when dropped in cold water. Pour fudge into buttered pan, and add remaining ingredients. Beat with wooden spoon until creamy. Spread on waxed paper to cool. Cut when firm.

Yields 25 one-inch squares

—**ELIZABETH P. deMONTMOLLIN,** *Columbia*

My family thinks no Christmas menu is complete without coconut cake.

—**MITTIE HATCH**

Columbia

CHRISTMAS COCONUT CAKE

1 white cake mix

1 14-ounce package shredded coconut, divided

1 cup sour cream

1½ cups sugar

1 8-ounce carton of Cool Whip topping

1 teaspoon almond flavoring

Bake cake mix according to package directions, using 3 round 9-inch cake pans. Mix one half of the coconut with sour cream, sugar, Cool Whip and almond flavoring. Spread between cake layers, on sides and on top of cake. Sprinkle remaining coconut on top and sides of cake. Let stand 8 hours in refrigerator before serving.

Serves 16–20

—**MITTIE HATCH,** *Columbia*

When there are small children, I enjoy hiding the presents in obvious places, like out on the deck in the snow. All the while I would be making lots of fudge for everyone to share. The children would be in awe as to how Santa could do that, never suspecting it was me, Aunt Sissy.

—**NORMA SORGEE**

Rock Hill

VANGIE'S SIX FLAVORED POUND CAKE

1 cup (2 sticks) butter or margarine

½ cup corn oil

3 cups granulated sugar

5 eggs

3 cups plus 2 tablespoons unsifted plain flour

1 teaspoon baking powder

1 cup milk

1 teaspoon vanilla extract

1 teaspoon lemon extract

1 teaspoon almond extract

1 teaspoon rum extract

1 teaspoon sherry extract

1 teaspoon brandy extract

Preheat oven to 325° F.

In a large bowl, cream butter, oil and sugar. Add eggs, one at a time, mixing well between each addition. In a separate bowl, sift together flour and baking powder. Alternate adding flour and milk to creamed mixture, beginning and ending with flour. Stir in flavorings last.

Turn dough into greased tube pan and bake for 1 hour and 15 to 30 minutes. Test for doneness with a toothpick. (This makes a very large cake.)

Serves 12–15

—**NORMA SORGEE,** *Rock Hill*

SMALL FINGER FRUIT CAKE

2 pounds candied pineapple
  (red and green)

2 pounds candied cherries (red and green)

1 pound whole pecans

4 cups all-purpose flour

4 level teaspoons baking powder

1 pinch salt

1 pound butter (4 sticks)

2 cups granulated sugar

10 eggs

1 tablespoon black walnut flavoring

2 tablespoons burgundy

Preheat oven to 300° F.

Start with all ingredients at room temperature. Chop fruit and nuts and set aside in large bowl. In another bowl, sift together flour, baking powder and salt. Using a handful or so of the flour, coat fruit and nuts, making sure they are well separated and not clumped together.

In large bowl, cream butter and sugar. Add eggs two at a time, beating well between each addition. Add remaining flour, flavoring and wine. Pour dough over floured fruit, and mix lightly but thoroughly.

Spoon dough into miniature cupcake pans with paper liners. Place a pan of water on bottom shelf of oven under the baking cakes, and bake for 2 hours and 20 minutes or until toothpick comes out clean.

Yields 4–6 dozen cakes

—**NELL VIRGINIA McMINN PETTY,** *Greenville*

This Small Finger Fruit Cakes recipe is from my mother, Nell Virginia McMinn Petty of Greenville. I found it on a torn envelope dated October 29, 1932. My family doesn't care for regular fruit cake, but they love this one.

—**ALLEENE KRACHT**
Columbia

SOUR CREAM POUND CAKE

1 cup (2 sticks) butter or margarine

3 cups granulated sugar

6 eggs

1 cup sour cream

3 cups all-purpose flour

¼ teaspoon soda

¼ teaspoon baking powder

3 teaspoons lemon or vanilla

1 teaspoon coconut flavoring

Preheat oven to 325° F.

Cream butter and sugar, and beat in one egg at a time. Add sour cream and mix well. In a separate bowl, sift together flour, baking soda and baking powder. Add flour to creamed mixture a little at a time, mixing well. Stir in the flavorings.

Bake in greased tube pan for 1 hour and 30 minutes, until golden brown and crusty on top.

ICING *(optional)*
Juice of 1 lemon
1 cups confectioners' sugar, sifted

Add lemon juice to sugar 1 tablespoon at a time. When icing is smooth enough to cover cake, don't add any more lemon juice. Spread while cake is still warm.

Serves 16–20

—**BETTY DENT,** *Columbia*

After Christmas Eve church services, we open gifts and have hot chocolate.

—**DORIS FEARRINGTON**
Columbia

MRS. M'S BREAD CRUMBS AND CUSTARD

Custard:

2 eggs

2 cups milk

1 cup sugar

1½ tablespoons vanilla flavoring

Bread Crumbs:

6 biscuits (or pie crust), crumbled

½ cup chopped pecans (or more, if you like)

4 tablespoons butter, melted

¼ cup sugar

To make custard: Beat eggs well and add milk and sugar. Cook over low heat, stirring constantly, until the consistency of buttermilk. Remove from heat, and add vanilla flavoring. Chill.

To make bread crumbs: Crumble biscuits on a cookie sheet and add pecans. Dribble melted butter on top. Sprinkle sugar over the crumbs and nuts, and stir to coat the crumbs well. Preheat oven to 325° F. Place in oven and toast slowly until golden brown.

Just before serving, place hot bread crumbs in a bowl and pour the cooled boiled custard over it.

Serves 12–15

—**JUDY MULLINAX,** *formerly of Jenkinsville*

LOLA'S BUTTERMILK CUSTARD

2 cups sugar

1 cup buttermilk

½ cup butter (1 stick), melted

3 tablespoons all-purpose flour

3 eggs

1 teaspoon vanilla

2 unbaked prepared pie shells

Preheat oven to 250° F.

Combine all ingredients, except pie shells, in a bowl, and mix with spoon or with a mixer at low speed until blended. Pour into two pie shells. Bake for 20 minutes at 250° F and then for 15 minutes at 450° F.

Serves approximatley 15

—**CHARLES A. DAVIS,** *West Columbia*

DIPPED NUTS AND CHERRIES

6 ounces semi-sweet chocolate chips or squares

25 whole nuts—pecans, walnuts, almonds (whatever you prefer)

1 8-ounce jar maraschino cherries, approximately 25 cherries

Melt chocolate in a saucepan over medium heat. Dip nuts into chocolate and place on waxed paper to dry. Dip cherries, including stems, and place on waxed paper to dry. Serve together in candy dish.

Makes 50 covered cherries and nuts

—**JOHN RUTLEDGE HOUSE INN,** *Charleston*

CHOCOLATE PECAN PIE

3 eggs, beaten
⅔ cup white corn syrup
⅔ cup sugar
1¼ cups pecan halves

¼ cup chocolate chips
1 teaspoon vanilla
¼ teaspoon salt
1 unbaked prepared pie crust

Preheat oven to 350° F.

In large bowl, combine all ingredients, except pie crust, and mix well. Pour filling into prepared pie crust and bake for 45 minutes. This is great served warm with vanilla ice cream.

Makes one 9-inch pie, serves 8–10

—**ERNESTINE CONNER,** *Orangeburg*

DAMSON PLUM PIE

1 quart jar pitted Damson plums
½ cup sugar (or more or less, to taste)
3 tablespoons cornstarch

2 cooked pie crusts
Cool Whip topping

In a sauce pan, heat plums (with juice) over medium heat. Add sugar and stir until dissolved. Remove a little of the juice from the sauce pan and mix with cornstarch until thickened. Add cornstarch mixture to plums and stir. Allow filling to cool, then pour into cooked pie crusts and refrigerate. Top with Cool Whip or real whipped cream. This makes a beautiful rich red colored pie.

Yields 12–16 slices

—**ANN E. KEETER,** *Columbia*

FERRELL'S PECAN PIE

3 eggs, beaten
1 cup granulated sugar
½ cup white Karo corn syrup
  (I like to use a little more)

4 tablespoons butter
1 teaspoon vanilla
1 cup pecan halves
1 unbaked prepared pie shell

Preheat oven to 350° F.

In a sauce pan, combine eggs, sugar, corn syrup, butter and vanilla, and stir over medium heat until butter melts. Add pecans and stir to blend well. Pour filling into an unbaked pie shell. Cook for about 40 minutes or until firm. Cool and serve.

Yields 8–10 slices

—**NORMA SORGEE,** *Rock Hill*

One very special Christmas Eve that I remember was when I was about ten years old. All the family gathered around in the living room, and because I was taking piano lessons at the time, I played for them. We read the Christmas story from the Bible and sung carols. Then my mother served her pound cake and custard. She had boiled the custard a little too long and it had curdled when she'd put it on the back porch to cool. I thought the custard tasted wonderful. It wasn't until later in life that I learned custard was supposed to be smooth. But it was never as good as my mother's.

—**DOT THOMPSON**
Greenville

My granddaughter is carrying on the tradition of baking pecan pies for family gatherings.

—**NORMA SORGEE**
Rock Hill

The library of the Governor's Mansion decorated for the holidays, Columbia

The Governor's Mansion

Two life-size toy soldiers stand at attention outside the Governor's Mansion during the holiday season, welcoming visitors to South Carolina's official state residence. Located in the heart of historic Columbia, the Governor's Mansion was built in 1855 as housing for officers of the Arsenal Military Academy. Fortunately, the building was spared during the Civil War when much of Columbia burned. In 1868 it became the official residence for the governor, and since then more than thirty chief executives and their families have lived here.

Christmas is a special time at the Governor's Mansion. In early December, the governor and first lady preside over the annual Christmas Open House, often greeting guests at the front door. Visitors are invited into the residence for refreshments and entertainment. Carolers, choirs, musicians, actors, and dancers perform both in the mansion and throughout the grounds and gardens. Children are always delighted by the elaborate gingerbread house, which takes Chef Bruce Sacino more than forty hours to bake and decorate.

For nearly twenty years the Columbia Garden Club has decorated the Governor's Mansion, using only fresh greenery. The South Carolina Tree Growers Association donates

two Christmas trees: one stands in the large drawing room, the other outside in the garden, decorated with food for South Carolina's feathered friends.

The nine-acre estate also includes two beautifully restored antebellum houses—the Lace House and the Caldwell-Boylston House—which are used for official functions as well. Many of South Carolina's state treasures are displayed here—traditional silver and china patterns, furniture, paintings, and historic documents. All three houses are open at Christmastime, each lavishly decorated to celebrate the season.

GINGERBREAD DOUGH
(For constructing a Gingerbread House)

2 cups molasses

1 cup vegetable oil

1 ¼ cups brown sugar

3 eggs

10 cups all-purpose flour

2 tablespoons allspice, ground

1 ½ tablespoons ginger, ground

1 tablespoon baking powder

Combine molasses, vegetable oil and sugar in a large stainless steel bowl. Add eggs, one at a time, stirring until blended after each addition. In a separate large bowl, combine flour, allspice, ginger and baking powder. Gradually add flour to molasses mixture, mixing well. Remove dough from bowl, wrap in plastic wrap, and refrigerate several hours or overnight.

Knead dough on a floured surface until it is smooth and free of cracks. With a rolling pin, roll out dough ¼ inch thick. With a sharp knife, cut out shapes according to your gingerbread house pattern.

Preheat oven to 350°F. Bake pieces or 15 minutes each. Allow to cool completely and let rest overnight to ensure hardness for construction.

ROYAL ICING

½ teaspoon cream of tartar

2 egg whites

2 cups or more confectioners' sugar

Place cream of tartar and egg whites in stainless steel bowl and mix on medium speed to form firm icing. Add more sugar as necessary (depending on size of eggs).

—CHEF BRUCE A. SACINO, *The Governor's Mansion, Columbia*

*The indoor Christmas tree includes
the first family's own decorations*

The night before Christmas

BAKED CURRIED FRUIT

1 15-ounce can peach halves	*Sauce*
1 16-ounce can pear halves	⅓ cup butter
1 8-ounce jar maraschino cherries	¾ cup brown sugar
1 20-ounce can pineapple chunks	2 tablespoons all-purpose flour
1 14-ounce can sliced apples or apple rings	1 cup fruit juice
	2 teaspoons curry powder

Drain fruit, reserving the juices for the sauce. Arrange fruit in a casserole dish. Combine sauce ingredients and cook in double boiler until thickened. Pour the sauce over fruit and refrigerate overnight.

Preheat oven to 325° F. Bake fruit for 15 minutes and serve. Can be served hot or cold.

Serves 12–15

—**ELIZABETH P. deMONTMOLLIN,** *Columbia*

Caesars Head State Park

VISITORS WILL BE
ADMITTED TO THE HOUSE
EVERY HALF HOUR
BEGINNING AT 10 AM
(1 PM SUNDAY)
LAST TOUR AT 4:30 PM
PLEASE PULL THE BELL.

Please
PULL BE

DECORATING SOUTH CAROLINA FOR CHRISTMAS

So many South Carolinians are avid gardeners that decorating for Christmas is often simply a matter of snipping flowers and greenery from their year-round gardens. The state's mild winters, particularly in the eastern half, produce all manner of flora, many of which bloom around the holidays. Magnolias, camellias, and nandina bushes flower in December, as does the popcorn tree—also known as the Chinese tallow tree because of its waxy foliage (in China it is called the Carolina tallow tree). Beautiful paper-white narcissus put forth their blossoms at this time of year, often growing in profusion around the foundations of old buildings.

Greenery is the basis for most Christmas decorating here, and the yards and woods of South Carolina are filled with many lovely species of native greens. Holly, deodara cedar, pine, smilax, boxwood, yews, balsam, crepe myrtle, variegated ivy, illicium, and cyprus are the most commonly used varieties. To this diversity of foliage South Carolinians artfully add accents such as pine cones, seed pods (okra and lotus), wheat or rice shafts, and the wispy, gray Spanish moss found shrouding the arms of great live oaks. According to Charleston gardener, floral arranger, and author Jan MacDougal, pretty much anything goes, as long as you can find it in the woods or take it out of your own yard.

Holiday doorway, Fountain Inn

The town of Fountain Inn has developed many holiday traditions throughout the years, created in the spirit of community and cooperation. Along with a live, narrated nativity pageant, each major street in town chooses a theme and each house decorates using that theme. Our street was "Jingle Bell Lane," and we made gold bells and hung them from all our trees.

—**MARY ABERCROMBIE**
Fountain Inn

Left: A Charleston exterior tastefully adorned with minimal decorations

Far left: A spray made of pittosporum, cedar, holly, wheat, gilded cones, and seed pods made by the Charleston Garden Club hangs on the front door of the Joseph Manigault House, Charleston

Nesbit House, Moncks Corner

My son, Captain Harley B. Hackett, III, a U.S. Air Force jet fighter pilot in Southeast Asia, has been missing in action since 1968. When Harley was in Cub Scouts, a project for each boy in his troop was to make a wooden Christmas bell for his mother. Harley cut it, painted and decorated it himself. It has become one of my dearest treasures, and I have used it as my front door decoration since 1968. For me, Christmas is love, family, friends, and memories —and keeping these in our hearts.

—REBECCA KNOBELOCH
Florence

Southern homes traditionally have a bouquet of greens in the house throughout the year. Around Thanksgiving people start decorating for Christmas, adding more greens and flowers, and fashioning arrangements of citrus fruits, with the oranges and lemons often studded with cloves. For Christmas, they simply replace the more perishable flowers and fruit within the existing greenery.

It is not unusual to find palmettos, boxwoods, magnolias, live oaks, and many other outdoor trees and bushes festooned with lanterns and lights during Christmas season. Inside the house, Christmas trees are usually scotch pine, cedar, or—most commonly—Fraser fir. Naturalist John Fraser first discovered the tree in the mountains of North Carolina. He called it the "she balsam," but it was later renamed in his honor. A part-time resident of Charleston, Fraser once operated a nursery-plantation on Johns Island, growing plants for sale in London. Today the Fraser fir is one of the most popular Christmas trees in the country.

Another holiday plant, the poinsettia, also has connections to South Carolina. While serving as ambassador to Mexico in 1824, Joel R. Poinsett discovered a brilliant flowering shrub. Knowing how gardeners in his hometown of Charleston so loved flowers, he brought it to their attention, and they promptly named it after him. South Carolinians like to place pots of poinsettias among the branches of their Christmas trees, along with magnolias and camellias, for a dramatic red, white, and green motif—creating with native plants the colors and spirit of Christmas.

Poinsettias in foyer, Fireproof Building, Charleston

Above: Garlands abound on a Summerville home
Right: A wreath made of local greenery, Cheraw

Natural Christmas Greens
Town Hall
Cheraw, South Carolina

A Cheraw Community Christmas

For historic Cheraw, decorating the town for Christmas is a community project. The Civic League Garden Club and the Four Seasons Garden Club join in the effort along with dozens of volunteers and town employees. The work begins the first of December when three large white pines trees and two huge cedars are cut down to provide the greenery for garlands and wreaths. Bushes and shrubs, planted for this project, are pruned to provide variety. The townspeople work together to fashion the natural greens into a dozen big wreaths and hundreds of feet of garland, which will all be adorned with with big red bows. When the decorations are done, they are hung on the town's historic and public buildings in plenty of time for the Optimist's Christmas parade, which follows a route that passes all the festive buildings.

Mountain laurel and white pine, Sumter National Forest

Each year during the first week of December, I help coordinate the making of natural greens for the Town of Cheraw. Two garden clubs, community volunteers, and town employees all work together for this massive project, putting natural wreaths and swags on the public and historic buildings and also the signs welcoming people to Cheraw. It's wonderful to see a community work together to keep a prized tradition alive.

—**CHERYL POSTLEWAIT**
Cheraw

Above: The Nathaniel Russell
House, Charleston
Right: Aiken Choral
Society's Home Tour

Left: Camillias add to the holiday
decor, Tabby Manse, Beaufort

Our Christmas season starts Thanksgiving weekend, when I decorate the house. My grown children now do the same. At Thanksgiving dinner I give each of the children a Christmas decoration for their homes, and each grandchild gets an ornament at their place at the table.

—**BETTY F. DENT**
Columbia

Joseph Manigault House, Charleston

The Joseph Manigault House

By the turn of the 19th century, Charleston had become an elegant and sophisticated city where wealthy landowners built town homes in the popular architectural styles of the day. Joseph Manigault and his wife, Charlotte Drayton, were no exception. Joseph Manigault, a member of the state legislature and a trustee of the College of Charleston, was an important figure in South Carolina. Having descended from French Huguenots who arrived in Charleston in the 1600s, Joseph had inherited vast land holdings from his grandfather. In 1803, he and Charlotte built a house on the corner of Meeting and John Streets. Joseph's brother Gabriel, a talented amateur architect, designed the Federal-style home.

Now owned by the Charleston Museum, the Manigault House has been carefully restored to its former splendor. According to recent research, it is likely that the family spent Christmas either at White Oak, their rice plantation outside of the city, or at Drayton Hall with Charlotte's family. No information exists on how the Manigault House might have been decorated for Christmas, so the Garden Club of Charleston creates arrangements using dozens of plants that would have been available in the first quarter of the 19th century. From the arched entryway to the elegant curving staircase, the house is adorned with native greenery, flowers, and fruit. Open to the public for tours, the historic Manigault House is especially popular during the Christmas season when it is bedecked in holiday regalia.

"I'm afraid it will tire you my dear sister to have a description of some of our X-mas boxes; all, I would not attempt. I will venture then to describe the handsomest of them. Mama gave each of us, that is, C. E. and myself, a pearl brooch…. The most handsomest present was a set of beads which Charles gave to Charlotte. I never saw anything like them before…. This amiable brother of ours gave me a very pretty clasp to confine my delicate waist. He gave Emma a gold thimble and Darling a pair of scissors."

—HENRIETTA MANIGAULT
in a letter to her sister, December 26, 1813.
(From the Manigault Collection, courtesy of the South Caroliniana Library, University of South Carolina.)

Holiday topiary, Joseph Manigault House

Middleton Place and Gardens was once the home of Henry Middleton, President of the First Continental Congress. America's oldest formal gardens, built in 1741, these grand terraces sweep up from the Ashley River, culminating in a pair of butterfly lakes. A restored rice mill stands at the edge of one of the lakes.

At the Henrietta Plantation north of Charleston, floral designer Jan MacDougal arranged camillias in a graceful decorative swan

Redcliffe Plantation

Redcliffe Plantation, a 1859 antebellum mansion in the classic Greek Revivalist style of architecture, was home to the Hammond family for 116 years. Many notable South Carolinians have lived there, including former governor John Henry Hammond and journalist John Shaw Billings. Every year the public is invited to a day-long Christmas event at historic Redcliffe. Storytellers, church choirs, and carolers provide the entertainment and guests join in for sing-alongs. A different theme is selected each year, relating to a particular period of history, and the mansion—still exhibiting the family furnishings—is decorated accordingly. Guests wander through the mansion, stroll the beautifully landscaped grounds, and enjoy the shade of a 140-year-old magnolia lane.

Redcliffe Plantation, Aiken

The VanderHorst House in Charleston was built in 1832 by Elias VanderHorst as his family's town residence; their plantation was on Kiawah Island, which was owned by the VanderHorsts.

A Thorntree Christmas

by Frances Ward, Williamsburgh Historical Society

"T'was the night before Christmas and all through the house..." A dramatic presentation of Clement Moore's classic story is given each holiday season during the Thorntree Christmas. The home is decorated with fresh fruit, smilax, and magnolia to recreate the feeling of Christmastide in the 18th century. Carolers sing by the soft glow of candlelight.

This annual wine and cheese party is hosted by members of the Williamsburgh County Historical Society, which was founded in 1967 to oversee the restoration of the historic home. Thorntree was originally the home of John Witherspoon, who arrived in Charleston in 1734 with a party of Irish immigrants on the ship *Good Intent.* James, his wife, Elizabeth, and their five children had come to America to seek freedom and fortune. James received a land grant of 300 acres along the Black River in the township of Williamsburgh, and the young family prospered. In 1749 they moved into their new home, Thorntree.

Discovering the house in sad disrepair, a South Carolina historian and an internationally known decorative arts scholar decided Thorntree should to be preserved, and they helped form the Williamsburgh County Historical Society. The house, which has since been relocated to Kingstree, was carefully restored and furnished with period pieces.

When the staff at Aiken Regional Medical Center noticed how much folks enjoyed the walking track around the lake, we decided to make an event out of it for the community. Every year at Christmas we invite local school and church groups to perform music by the beautifully lit Christmas tree in front of the hospital. We always have plenty of hot apple cider, hot chocolate, cookies, and candied apples. Santa Claus makes a special appearance to greet the small children, and a visit to the "North Pole" booth is rewarded with a keepsake ornament for the family and a surprise memento for the children. During Christmas at the lake, we also take the opportunity to collect toys for the needy by coordinating the Christmas Toy Drive for the Salvation Army.

—Anonymous

A Garden Wonderland

HOPELAND GARDENS, AIKEN

Ten of thousands of twinkling lights and sparkling snowflakes adorn the ancient oaks, cedars, and magnolias at Hopeland Gardens, a holiday wonderland for young and old alike.

Bequeathed to the citizens of Aiken by Mrs. C. Oliver Iselin, this impressive fourteen-acre estate, where the Iselin Mansion once stood, has been converted into splendid public gardens. Sandy paths meander through the grounds, winding among the towering trees and lush landscaping.

For the last two weeks in December, Hopeland Gardens is the center of the city's Christmas celebrations. Local musical groups perform holiday songs as families and friends stroll among reindeer, poinsettias, ice skaters, swans, angels, and many other enchanting shapes.

Adjacent to Hopeland Gardens is Rye Patch, donated to the city by the family of Mrs. Dorothy Goodyear Rogers, and now used for Christmas parties, receptions, and other special events. A holiday craft show is held here one weekend in December, and the building remains open for public viewing during the entire Christmas in Hopeland festival.

Touring Hopeland Gardens

Heard from Heaven Today

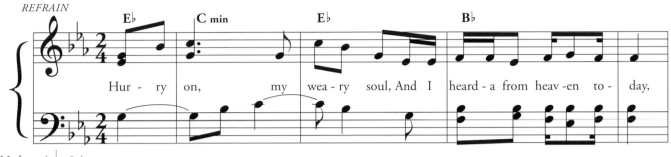

REFRAIN

Hur - ry on, my wea - ry soul, And I heard - a from heav -en to - day,

Moderate (♩ = 84)

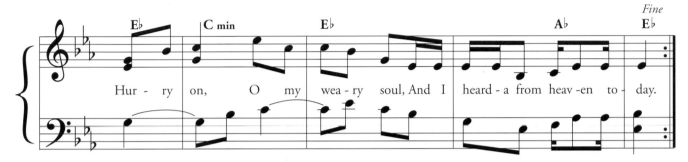

Hur - ry on, O my wea - ry soul, And I heard - a from heav -en to - day.

Fine

STANZA

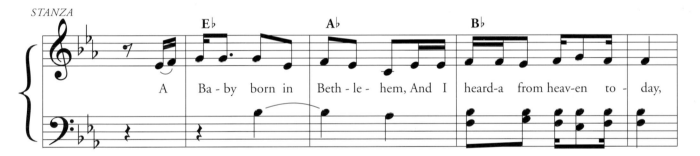

A Ba - by born in Beth - le - hem, And I heard-a from heav-en to - day,

D. C. without pause

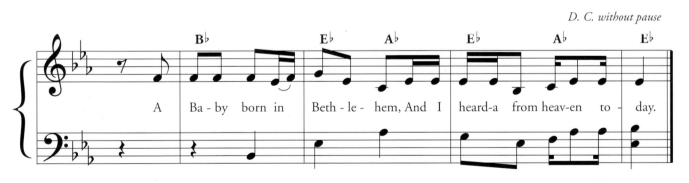

A Ba - by born in Beth - le - hem, And I heard-a from heav-en to - day.

Alternate Refrain:

Travel on, my weary soul,

And I heard-a from heaven today,

Travel on, O my weary soul,

And I heard-a from heaven today,

2. The bell is a-ringing in the other bright world,

And I heard-a from heaven today,

The bell is a-ringing in the other bright world,

And I heard-a from heaven today,

Refrain:

3. The trumpet sounds in the other bright land, *etc.*

Sunset over the marsh, Hobcaw Barony, near Georgetown

*Our favorite tradition is rambling
through the woods on our farm to
find the perfect Christmas tree.*

—MRS. T. LLOYD GARRETT
Fountain Inn

Christmas tree farm, near New Prospect

*Picking out a tree at Toogoodoo Christmas Tree Park,
Younges Island*

When I was growing up, we would get our tree about two weeks before Christmas. At that time there was no place to buy a tree, so my father and one of my brothers would go to the woods and cut one down. Mother always wanted a cedar tree, so they knew better than to bring home a pine. We didn't have any lights to go on the tree, but we did have a few ornaments and we made some too. After a few days our house would begin to smell of cedar—a wonderful smell that always reminds me of Christmas.

—DOT THOMPSON, Greenville

We love to go to the Christmas tree farm every year to look for just the right tree. Then we cut it down and go home to decorate it.

—HEATHER LOWDER
Columbia

*We always have a live tree at Christmas, which we plant
in our yard after the holidays. My husband and children
go together to pick the tree, which is a special event for
them. This past year our only married child called his dad
to be sure he would be included. He picked out a tree for
him and his new bride while my husband got one for us.
It was wonderful to see this tradition being passed on.*

—REBECCA CHASON, *Ballentine*

CHRISTMAS ON IRIS DRIVE

by Tommie Ward, Florence

T he first neighborhood Christmas party on Iris Drive in Florence was nearly 35 years ago. Each resident of the street decorated an outdoor Christmas tree with tin can lids. A cookout was held on the median, and Santa arrived by fire truck.

The tradition continues today, with about 25 households participating, only now we use colored lights to decorate the trees. Next to each tree is a wooden snowman with the last name of the household painted on it. On the first Saturday of December, late in the afternoon, the street is blocked off to traffic, and all the neighbors gather in the median for a cookout and Christmas carols. One of the original residents of Iris Drive sings "Silent Night" in German. The children play excitedly in the streets as they anticipate the arrival of Santa—now in a convertible.

After the party, any leftover food is taken to the Salvation Army. The barricades are then removed from the street, and the procession of cars begins. Hundreds of cars travel down the street as people come to see the decorations. The Iris Drive Christmas party is a wonderful time to share the Christmas spirit with our neighbors.

During the holidays we always have a tree ornament contest. Friends and family who visit us at Christmas try to guess how many ornaments are on the tree. When the tree is taken down, the ornaments are counted, and the winner receives a gift that we buy on sale in January.

—DOUG AND ALLEENE KRACHT
Columbia

Antique dolls sit beneath a tree hung with handmade ornaments, Gramling

Handmade ornaments

THE CHRISTMAS PIG
by Gretchen D. Rhinehardt, Summerville

Christmas traditions are as varied and unusual throughout the South as anywhere in the world. Without our own customs and celebrations Christmas would be only a date on our December calendar. Many trim their trees with heirlooms, bows, tinsel, garland, candy canes, silver bells, even teething rings and tiny shoes. We've added an ornament to our tree that to some may seem a bit unusual, but it has become a holiday tradition in our house. In fact, it isn't really Christmas until the pig is hung.

It all began Christmas 1977 when I received the "pig" as a gift. My daughter Chassity was four and attending kindergarten. Christmas was just around the corner, and the teacher asked the children to select an ornament they could make and give their mother as a gift. Some selected angels or stars, others picked Santas or candy canes. We are still unable to explain why Chassity selected a pig, but she did. She designed, shaped, and painted the most hideous pig. Made of plaster of Paris and painted blue, it was so ugly you couldn't help but love it. It came complete with hanger, ready to be hung on the Christmas tree.

We hung it on the tree that Christmas and every Christmas since. We've had all kinds of trees through the years, and each year a new decorating theme. Regardless of the motif, the tree is never complete without the pig, nor has Christmas really arrived at our house until "the pig has been hung." This endearing personal tradition has become as much a part of our Christmas as celebrating the birth of baby Jesus, Santa Claus, or opening presents on Christmas morning.

We give our children a new ornament each Christmas—something symbolic of their past year.

—DOUG AND ALLEENE KRACHT
Columbia

Sand dollars and seashells decorate a Lowcountry tree

Every year as we unpack our Christmas ornaments and hang them on the tree, we tell where each one came from and the story behind it. It brings to mind the wonderful memories of our lives together as a family. Each one is treasured, whether it's made of paper or crystal.

—MRS. TERESA KLEEBLATT
Fountain Inn

Even though my children
are all grown, they come
home sometime during the
holidays, and Christmas
is celebrated on whatever
day we are all together.
I still put stockings up,
not only for my children
but also for all the grandchildren and all their pets.

—**SANDRA DERRICK**
Seneca

We have a holiday table-
cloth that each person in the
family draws on with perma-
nent markers, making holiday
designs. Later, I embroider it.
We have done this for about
six years, and the tablecloth
is now quite colorful.

—**BETTY L. KOMEGERY**
Columbia

*Stockings hung by the fire
with care, Columbia*

Father Christmas in an authentic Victorian costume, Fireproof Building, Charleston

The Fireproof Building

The magnificent Fireproof Building in Charleston is one of the finest works by famed South Carolinian architect Robert Mills, designer of the Washington Monument. The original purpose of the Fireproof Building was to house state records. Today it is home to the South Carolina Historical Society. Located on the corner of Meeting and Chalmers Streets, it has been a Charleston landmark since 1827.

Each year at Christmas, the Historical Society opens the building to the public, placing its priceless historical treasures and dramatic architecture on view for all who wish to visit. A building of such grand proportions is not easy to decorate, but the staff works for weeks ahead of time to affix mountains of natural greens, fresh-cut from Charleston-area plantations. The main staircase—soaring, free-standing stone slabs that rise dramatically upward for three stories—is draped in garlands of greenery and red bows. A spectacular fourteen-foot Christmas tree is heavily laden with some 7,000 lights and decorated with more than 400 antique, hand-blown glass ornaments on loan to the society from a private collection.

In the glow of hundreds of candles, Christmas at the Fireproof Building is a lavish Victorian celebration, complete with carolers, string quartets, choirs, and a visit from Father Christmas. It combines the history and architecture of South Carolina with the beauty of the Christmas season.

Every ornament on my tree has some special meaning to me, signifying places I've visited or people I have known. I hang them all, especially the ones that my children made when they were in kindergarten.

—SANDRA DERRICK, Seneca

Hospice trees, Florence

The annual Hospice Tree Program of McLeod Regional Medical Center has become one of Florence's official beginnings of the holiday season. Since 1986, in a tradition of community spirit, private support, and genuine caring, the McLeod Foundation has sponsored "A Light for Someone You Love," which benefits McLeod Hospice of the Pee Dee. Families and friends are offered the opportunity to illuminate a tree or a light in memory of a loved one or dear friend. Last year, 31 trees were donated and thousands of lights were illuminated as approximately 300 family members and friends attended.

—JOAN HARRISON PAVY, *Florence*

Decorating a "Children's Tree"

I was the youngest of four children. The one next to me was nine years older, so I grew up very spoiled and pampered. Some would say I was a brat. When I was about five or six years old, I can remember my sister, who was in her teens, used to write letters to Santa Claus for me. Since we didn't have central heat we always had an open fire, and she would send the letters up the chimney to Santa. Sometimes she would write that I had been bad and that Santa should bring a bag of switches. Other times she would write that I had been good and send a list of my wishes.

—DOT THOMPSON
Greenville

THE GREAT AWAKENING
by Ernestine Frederick Conner, Charleston

*I*t was many, many years ago, the Christmas after my twelfth birthday. Christmas was quite effervescent at my home with four older boys and a baby brother. I was the only girl. After opening the presents, eating breakfast, and thanking God for his many blessings, I was allowed to go to the neighbor's house to play with their three girls.

As typical of South Carolina Christmases, the weather was mild, and we were sitting under a giant oak tree sharing our dolls and all the accessories that came with them. I was the oldest among the four of us, and we were all having a good, giggling, hilarious time. My friends' mother came out to check on us and she asked what Santa had brought me. I told her. She said, "You don't know who Santa is, do you, Ernestine?" I was speechless. I had never really thought about it. Why Santa was Santa, of course!

"Ernestine," she said. "Your mamma and daddy is." What did she say? "Your mamma and daddy is Santa Claus." I was devastated. Her daughters began to laugh and say, "Stine, you didn't know!" Well, I didn't know. I was crushed, humiliated, embarrassed, and some other words I couldn't think of at the time. I ran home to ask my mom. She confirmed it. My brothers confirmed it. I only wanted to know one thing, why hadn't someone told me? Christmas was never quite the same after the "great awakening."

I remember having to go to bed early on Christmas Eve so that Santa would come. We were told if we peeked, Santa would spit tobacco juice in our eyes. I would lie awake with my eyes shut tight for what seemed like hours. I'd finally fall asleep, only to be awakened by the aroma of fresh oranges and apples. I knew then that it was safe to open my eyes because Santa had visited our house.

—PECOLIA ELLISON
Columbia

My brother and I would always start looking through the catalogs and begin making our lists at least four months before Christmas.

—JENNIFER PRINCE
Irmo

When we were kids, my younger brother and I always slept in the same bed on Christmas Eve, waiting for Santa to come.

—KEVIN PARKER
Union

On Christmas morning we read the Christmas story in Luke and say a prayer. Then we listen to Christmas music and take turns opening our gifts one at a time. After breakfast—the same one every year—we open our stockings.

—JACQUE HUDGENS
Columbia

Twenty feet tall and decorated in style, Fountain Inn

LOOKING BACK WITH A LAUGH

by Mittie Hatch, Columbia

Our four boys have always seen to it that the night before Christmas was never long, and that Christmas day dawned early. We would gather in the living room around the lighted tree and begin the day by hearing again from the Bible of that first Christmas gift. Then we would pray around the circle, giving thanks for the gift of God's Son. The boys' prayers were very brief and to-the-point! And then it was time for the stockings, the presents, the hugs of gratitude, the joyous confusion of that very special day.

The years passed, the sons grew up, married, had families of their own, and we were scattered far and wide. Our second son, Allen, and his family went to Quito, Ecuador, where he worked as an engineer for a missionary radio station.

One December day just before Christmas when most of the extended family was together again in Columbia, we tuned in a shortwave program that Allen was broadcasting from Quito. The program was beamed to ham operators in the States, so it was in English. As Allen played familiar Christmas recordings and chatted on the air, he began to reminisce of his childhood memories of Christmas in Columbia. He told of our custom of reading and praying together on Christmas morning, and then with a chuckle added, "I really appreciate my family, but I think we would have gotten more out of it if they had let us tackle our gifts first."

Satin and pearls

When we were young, we would watch the Santa report from Joe Penner on WIS/TV. One Christmas my brother and I wouldn't go to sleep, until we heard on the TV that Santa was flying over Irmo. We screamed and quickly ran to jump into bed.

—JENNIFER PRINCE
Irmo

When all six children were still living at home, the youngest child would open gifts first and then we would work our way up to the oldest. That way each child got individual attention. My husband always kept a written record of each gift as it was opened so we would get our thank you notes right. Our children and grandchildren still spend Christmas with us, and we still start with the youngest opening the gifts.

—JOAN DAVIS
Greenville

Our family celebrated its first Christmas together in 1996, when our daughter Brianna Catherine was seven months old. We started a special Christmas Eve tradition, with Santa bringing our little girl her first gift—a pair of pajamas, just like he used to bring me when I was little a girl. She also received a copy of THE NIGHT BEFORE CHRISTMAS, which was passed around the room so that grandparents, parents, uncles, and friends could each read a page to her. We plan to read it every Christmas Eve as our own family tradition for getting ready for the arrival of Santa Claus.

—AMY WOOD, *WSPA News Channel 7, Spartanburg*

A RURAL CELEBRATION
by Dr. Thalia J. Coleman, formerly of Lake View

*A*ll our friends in Lake View decorated their houses elaborately, but we had the most elaborate decorations of all. Over every window and door and all through the house were holly branches from the woods. The only things that were store-bought were the little twinkling lights and an occasional glass ball. A week or two before Christmas, Mother and all seven of us children went into the woods to cut down a pine tree. It was a happy time, as we all participated in selecting the tree and bringing it home. We couldn't afford a real tree stand, so we set it up in a bucket of sand and then proceeded to decorate every inch of that tree. We strung popcorn, made paper chains and paper cut-outs, and then hung it all, along with anything else that looked attractive. Occasionally we were able to buy a box of tinsel.

Mother and Daddy didn't place gifts under the tree because they loved to play Santa Claus, handing out the gifts one by one. We each received one gift unless there was a collective toy for all of us, like a bicycle or a Radio Flyer wagon. As we grew older, we were pressed into playing Santa for the younger children, so we held out for years pretending that we believed in Santa Claus, because we knew if we didn't it meant the end of the toys.

There were two bushel baskets under the tree, one filled with apples and the other with oranges. There was also a large bag of nuts and another of candy. On Christmas morning, after Santa, we were each given a large brown paper sack, and the apples, oranges, nuts, and candy were divided among us. Most of us ate our goodies right away, but I remember my sister Diane always managed to hoard hers and was eating in front of six envious faces long after our sacks were empty. Children today have such easy access to fruit and candy that they cannot appreciate how special these once-a-year treats were to us.

Since my children were babies, we have sent a picture Christmas card to our friends and relatives. Several years ago I framed all the Christmas cards from over the years, and gave them as gifts to my grown children. They were all thrilled. They said it was one of the best presents ever—to see their lives from babyhood to adulthood in one big framed picture.

—BETTY F. DENT
Columbia

Among the wrapped gifts under the tree there is one with a tag that reads, "To the Yoders, From Santa." After dinner on Christmas Eve we open just one gift—the one from Santa. It is always a game that we sit down and play that night. We've acquired a great collection of games this way. Some are winners and some are duds, but either way we have a lot of fun playing the new game on Christmas Eve.

—HELEN YODER
Greenville

I remember that we always got one Christmas toy for everyone to enjoy—like a dog that did flips, or something equally as silly.

**—NELL VIRGINIA
MCMINN PETTY**
Greenville

Santa's helpers

A mantle village,
Fountain Inn

A MODEST CHRISTMAS PROPOSAL
by Mary Wood Beasley, First Lady of South Carolina

One Christmas memory that will be forever etched in my mind takes me back to a barn, where the smell of hay, sweet feed, and leather filled the air. The horses curiously poked their velvet noses over the stalls, nostrils smoking like chimneys in the cold December night.

We had chosen our favorite place to exchange gifts. We had agreed to only spend $10 on each other's present, because we had "adopted" a family and spent our Christmas money on them.

I gave him a picture of us in a plastic frame. We laughed at it. Then it was his turn. He had been hiding his present. I watched him stroll around the barn, and I admired, as always, his complete self-assurance. Time seemed to stand still. My face was hot, and my heart was beating so loudly I was sure he could hear it. Suddenly, as if tackled by a 350-pound linebacker, something took his breath away, and his eyes sort of rolled around as if he was dizzy. Then he fell to his knees with his gift in hand and asked me to m-m-m-marry him! I did.

The Toy Maker

Santa brought him a jigsaw when he was eight years old, and that's when Buddy Easler became a toy maker. Mostly self-taught, Buddy began by making playpens and cradles for his sisters' dolls. Then pretty soon he was making them for all the girls in the neighborhood. He attributes his first paying job (cutting Styrofoam for florists, before machines did that sort of thing) to the skills he learned while woodworking.

Now Buddy and his wife, Susan, have two grandchildren who are the beneficiaries of Buddy's craft. He made them handmade cars, wooden tricycles, and fabulous rocking horses inlaid with eight different kinds of wood. The girl had cradles and playpens, just like her great aunts.

Buddy makes toys for the fun of it, working mostly evenings and weekends. His recently expanded wood shop turns out toys and also decoys and real baby cradles, among other items. If someone wants a one-of-a-kind piece, it's liable to take six to seven months, depending on how busy he is, since he is only a one-man operation.

A few years ago, he decided his granddaughter needed a full-sized playhouse for Christmas, but that was too much for even Buddy to complete in the two weeks left before December 25. He commandeered his friends and neighbors to help on the project, and then he had to rent a flatbed truck to move it. "That's what Christmas is all about," he'll tell you. "Those grandkids."

A few years ago some Columbia "neighbors"—the Campbells—heard about Buddy's toys and wanted some as handcrafted Christmas decorations for their house—the Governor's Mansion. The next occupants of the house continued the tradition. And that's how Buddy Easler became known throughout South Carolina as "The Toy Maker."

My twelve-year-old daughter generally makes her own Christmas presents, laboring long and lovingly over each one. My eight-year-old son is just interested in what he's going to get. On Christmas morning, we always sing "Joy to the World" as we go downstairs. There is always an embarrassing number of presents under the tree, which we open slowly, one at a time, so we can savor each one and make it last longer.

—CLARE FRIST
Greenville

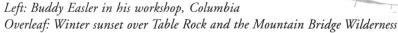

Left: Buddy Easler in his workshop, Columbia
Overleaf: Winter sunset over Table Rock and the Mountain Bridge Wilderness

After church Christmas Eve, we have
a boxed shrimp meal with chips.

—ALLEENE KRACHT
Columbia

*At the historic Elliott House Inn
we decorate two real trees in the
courtyard with white magnolias
and red poinsettias. On Christmas
morning we serve our guests a
special Christmas breakfast and
give each one an ornament as
a gift.*

*—Management of the
Elliott House Inn, Charleston*

Shrimp boat, Georgetown

DEVILED CRAB

1 pound crab meat, fresh or canned	4 hard-boiled eggs, grated
1 ½ cups cracker or bread crumbs	½ cup mustard
½ cup (1 stick) butter or margarine, melted	1 tablespoon mayonnaise
2 raw eggs, beaten	1 tablespoon hot sauce
2 stalks celery, diced	Dash of Worcestershire sauce
1 large onion, grated	Dash of soy sauce
1 medium bell pepper, finely chopped	Black pepper to taste

Preheat oven to 350° F.

If using fresh crab meat, shred the meat then pick over well to remove any cartilage and shell. If using canned crab, drain juice from can, flake meat with fork and pick over well.

Mix all ingredients in a large bowl. Fill cleaned crab shells, or foil backs, with crab meat mixture. Bake for 30 to 40 minutes. Sprinkle paprika on top.

Makes 2 dozen

—**MARGARET HAMILTON BROWN,** *Charleston*

Christmas morning is a time that the whole family gets together for a big breakfast, which is not possible during the rest of the year. We have a special breakfast casserole, pancakes, bacon, good breads, and scones and tea.

—**REBECCA CHASON**
Ballentine

CRAB DIP

1 8-ounce can crab meat	2 tablespoons horseradish
1 cup mayonnaise	2 tablespoons French dressing
1 cup grated sharp Cheddar cheese	1 tablespoon lemon juice

Drain juice from can, flake crab meat with fork and pick over well to remove any cartilage or shell. Mix all ingredients together. Serve with crackers.

Serves 16–20

—**BETTY DENT,** *Columbia*

On Christmas morning we have a formal breakfast, using all the Christmas china. Afterward, while we're still at the table, we each open a gift given by an immediate family member.

—**GENEVA B. FINNEY**
Orangeburg

OYSTER PIE

1 ½ pints oysters, fresh shucked or in a jar	2 cups milk
1 8-ounce package saltine crackers	1 teaspoon Worcestershire sauce
2 tablespoons butter or margarine, cut up	¼ teaspoon each salt and pepper
2 eggs, beaten (or egg substitute)	

Preheat oven to 350° F.

Drain and rinse oysters. Break saltines into large crumbs and cover the bottom of a 2-quart casserole with a layer of crumbs. Place a layer of oysters on top of saltines and dot with butter. Repeat layers of saltines, oysters and butter until there are three layers. Crumble saltines on top.

Combine eggs, milk, Worcestershire sauce, salt and pepper, and mix well. Pour over casserole and dot with butter. Milk mixture should cover saltines and oysters.

Bake for 50 minutes or until set in middle.

Serves 8–10

—**DORIS B. FEARRINGTON,** *Columbia*

An elegant holiday party table, Columbia

SAUSAGE AND CHEDDAR BISCUITS

5 tablespoons vegetable shortening	1½ cups grated cheddar cheese
2 cups self-rising flour	1 pound mild or hot ground sausage
⅔ cup milk	

Preheat oven to 425° F.

Using pastry blender, blend vegetable shortening into flour, then add milk and mix. Turn dough out onto a floured surface and knead. With a rolling pin, roll the dough until it is about one inch thick. Sprinkle grated cheese on top of dough.

Cook sausage until browned and drain off grease. Place cooked meat in food processor and grind into small crumbly pieces. Layer sausage on top of grated cheese.

Cut dough with biscuit cutter and place the rounds on an ungreased cookie sheet. Bake 10 to 12 minutes or until golden brown.

Makes 2 dozen biscuits

—**TERESA KLEEBLATT,** *Fountain Inn*

BISCUITS WITH HOT SHERRIED FRUIT

Biscuits

2 cups self-rising flour	⅓ cup Crisco shortening (Grandmama would use lard)
¼ teaspoon baking soda	1 cup buttermilk

Preheat oven to 450° F.

Sift together self-rising flour and baking soda. Add Crisco to flour, cutting with pastry blender. Add buttermilk and mix only until just moistened. Turn dough out onto floured surface, and knead about 5 times, or until dough is not sticky. Pat dough into ¾-inch thickness, and cut with a biscuit cutter.

Place biscuits on hot, greased baking pan (an iron skillet is best), with the sides of the biscuits touching. Bake 10 to 12 minutes until golden brown.

HOT SHERRIED FRUIT

1 16-ounce can pineapple chunks	½ cup light brown sugar
1 16-ounce can peaches	1 tablespoon cinnamon
1 16-ounce can pears	1 tablespoon cornstarch
½ cups cream sherry, or to taste	¼ cup cold water

Reserve the juice from all cans of fruit, and chop fruit into chunks. Put fruit and juices in 2-quart sauce pan, and heat gently over medium heat until fruit is soft. Add sherry, brown sugar and cinnamon, stirring occasionally until warm and the consistency of syrup.

In a small bowl, mix cornstarch and cold water and stir until smooth. Add cornstarch mixture to hot fruit and stir until blended. Cook until thick.

Split biscuits in half, or leave them whole, and spoon the sherried fruit on top.

Makes 12–14 biscuits

—**LINDA BISHOP,** *John Rutledge House Inn, Charleston*

MACARONI AND CHEESE

1½ cups macaroni noodles

½ cup margarine, cut up

1½ cups shredded medium sharp
  cheddar cheese

3 eggs, beaten

1 12-ounce can evaporated milk

Seasoning salt

Salt and pepper

Paprika

Preheat oven to 375° F.

Cook macaroni according to package directions, adding salt and pepper to the water.
Drain and add margarine, stirring until melted. Place noodles in casserole dish.

Combine remaining ingredients and mix well. Pour over noodles. Add a little regular
milk to mixture to keep it loose enough so it doesn't stick to the sides of the casserole.

Bake for about 45 minutes. Increase temperature to 400° F and cook for approximately
30 minutes more, or until macaroni is brown on top. Test for doneness in middle with
toothpick. This dish is cooked firm, so that a sliced piece will stand on a plate.

Serves 12–15

—**BARBARA AND WAYNE SUMPTER,** *Columbia*

TUNA MOLD

2 6- or 7-ounce cans tuna

2 chopped hard-boiled eggs

½ cup chopped green olives

1 tablespoon finely chopped onion

½ cup cold water

2 envelopes plain Knox gelatin

2 cups mayonnaise

Drain tuna well, break up with a fork, and add eggs, olives and onion. In a
measuring cup with ½ cup cold water, soften gelatin for several minutes, then place
the measuring cup in a saucepan filled with hot tap water to fully dissolve the gelatin.
Cool slightly and add to tuna along with mayonnaise (I always use Duke's mayonnaise).
Mix well.

Pour tuna mixture into fish-shaped or other mold pan that has been sprayed with
Pam. Cover with plastic wrap and refrigerate until firm. This dish can be made several
days ahead, but do not freeze. Unmold just prior to serving.

Makes 20 servings

—**BOOG HENDERSON,** *Spartanburg*

STRING BEANS WITH SOUR SAUCE

1 13½-ounce can string beans
1½ tablespoons butter
1 small onion, chopped fine
⅔ cup half and half

½ cup sugar
1 tablespoon all-purpose flour
¼ cup vinegar
½ teaspoon salt

Heat the string beans and then drain the liquid. Melt butter and sauté onion until translucent. Add the cream, sugar, flour, vinegar and salt, and stir until the sugar is dissolved and the sauce thickens slightly. Place the beans in a serving dish, pour the sauce on top and serve.

When I prepare this recipe, I often use fresh green beans, but frozen or canned beans work just as well. Since we like a lot of sauce, I usually double the amount of sauce. When I want to be fancy, I sprinkle almonds on top.

Serves 8–10

—ALLEENE KRACHT, *Columbia*

Dining Room, The Nathaniel Russell House, Charleston

ZUCCHINI PIE

4 cups thinly sliced zucchini
1 cup chopped onion
¼ to ½ cup margarine
2 eggs, beaten
½ cup freshly chopped parsley (or 2 tablespoons parsley flakes)
½ teaspoon salt
¼ teaspoon basil
¼ teaspoon oregano
¼ teaspoon garlic powder
1½ to 2 cups shredded mozzarella cheese
1 unbaked prepared pie crust

Preheat oven to 375° F.

In a large sauce pan, cook zucchini, onion and margarine over medium heat until mixture boils. Remove from heat. Add remaining ingredients, except pie crust, and stir until well mixed. Spoon filling into prepared pie crust. Bake for 18 to 20 minutes, or until the center is set.

Serves 8–10

—ERNESTINE CONNER, *Orangeburg*

LITTLE MOTHER'S FRENCH DRESSING

½ cup vegetable oil

¼ cup vinegar

1 small onion, grated

⅓ cup ketchup

½ cup sugar

1 teaspoon paprika

1 teaspoon celery seed

1 teaspoon prepared mustard

1 teaspoon salt

In a blender, combine oil, vinegar and onion and blend well. Combine ketchup and sugar in a mixer and mix well. Add blended ingredients to mixer, and beat for 3 minutes, gradually adding the spices.

Store dressing in a glass bottle, to which you may want to add a clove of garlic.

Yields about 1 cup

—**ALLEENE KRACHT,** *Columbia*

We quadruple the recipe and give decorated bottles of dressing to our friends as gifts. They now expect it every Christmas, and don't let us slip up.

— **ALLEENE KRACHT**
Columbia

SWEET POTATOES WITH SLICED ORANGES

2 large sweet potatoes,
  peeled and sliced to ¼ inch

½ cup butter (1 stick), cut up

4 tablespoons dark brown sugar

Salt to taste

1 orange, sliced thin

Place sweet potatoes, butter and brown sugar in large sauce pan, cover and cook over medium-low heat for 20 minutes. Salt potatoes to taste and arrange orange slices on top. Cook for another 15 minutes. Serve hot, garnished with extra orange slices and parsley.

Serves 6–8

—**CHEF ANDRÈ,** *Beaufort, prepared for The Rhett House Inn*

CRANBERRY SALAD

4 cups fresh cranberries, finely chopped

1 apple, finely chopped

1 cup chopped pecans

1 tablespoon lemon juice

Rind of one orange, grated

1 6-ounce box cherry Jell-O

1 cup boiling water

1 cup sugar

2 cups cold water

In a large bowl, combine cranberries, apples, pecans, lemon juice, and orange rind. In another bowl dissolve cherry Jell-O in boiling water. Add sugar and still until dissolved. Add cold water.

Pour Jell-O into bowl with fruit and mix well. Transfer to 9 x 14 glass dish or into individual molds. Refrigerate until congealed.

Makes 12 servings

—**DORIS FEARRINGTON,** *Columbia*

BLUEBERRY SALAD

2 small packages (3-ounce size) blackberry Jell-O

2 cups hot water

1 16-ounce can blueberries, drained

1 8-ounce can crushed pineapple, drained

1 cup fruit juice, reserved from pineapple and blueberries

Topping

1 8-ounce package cream cheese, softened

1 cup sour cream

½ cup sugar

1 teaspoon vanilla

½ cup chopped pecans or walnuts

To make salad, dissolve Jell-O in hot water. Add blueberries and pineapple and 1 cup of reserved juice. Pour into 9 x 9 glass baking dish. Cover and refrigerate until congealed.

To make topping, beat cream cheese in mixer on medium speed until smooth. Add remaining ingredients and mix well. Spread on top of congealed Jell-O mixture.

Serves 12–15

—**JUDY L. LOWDER,** *Columbia*

A Victorian Christmas tree,
Fountain Inn

CARROT, ZUCCHINI & APPLE MUFFINS

2 cups all-purpose flour

1 cup sugar

2 cups grated carrots

1 cup grated zucchini

1 golden delicious apple,
  cored and finely chopped

¾ cup golden raisins

¾ cup shredded coconut

½ cup almonds, coarsely chopped

2 teaspoons baking soda

2 teaspoons grated orange peel

1 tablespoon cinnamon

1 teaspoon vanilla

¾ teaspoon salt

1 cup vegetable oil

3 large eggs

Preheat oven to 375° F.

Mix all ingredients, except eggs and oil, in large bowl. In a smaller bowl, beat eggs and oil together. Stir oil and eggs into flour mixture and mix well.

Spoon ¼ cup batter into each cup of a muffin pan with paper liners. Bake for 25 minutes. Serve warm or at room temperature.

Makes 24 muffins

—**JOHN RUTLEDGE HOUSE INN,** *Charleston*

RUSSIAN TEA

3 sticks cinnamon

1 teaspoon whole cloves

2 cups water

8 tea bags, regular strength

1 ½ cups sugar

2 cups orange juice

½ cup lemon juice

8 cups water

Boil cinnamon and cloves in 2 cups water. Then steep tea bags in the mixture for about 10 minutes. Add sugar and stir until dissolved. Add orange juice, lemon juice and 8 cups water. Serve hot.

Make 13 one-cup servings

—**SARA PETTY,** *Columbia*

HOT CRANBERRY CIDER

1 ½ quarts cranberry juice

3 quarts apple juice

½ cup light brown sugar

½ teaspoon salt

4 cinnamon sticks

1 ½ teaspoons whole cloves

Pour cranberry and apple juices into a 5-quart pot. Add brown sugar and salt, and heat until dissolved.

Put cinnamon and cloves in cheesecloth and let steep in juice for at least 1 hour (may even be left in while serving). Heat thoroughly; the longer it heats, the spicier it becomes.

Makes 24 6-ounce servings.

—**CHEF BRUCE A. SACINO,** *The Governor's Mansion, Columbia*

Rhett House Inn

In the early 1800s Southern aristocrat Thomas Rhett and his wife, Caroline, likely sat on their veranda and watched the Spanish moss sway in the gentle sea breezes. The coastal town of Beaufort, an enchanting and highly cultured place, was home to many wealthy planters who spent part of the year in town and the rest of the year on their plantations, where they grew rice. When Union troops claimed Beaufort during the Civil War, the planters abandoned their town homes and fled to their plantations.

The Rhett House passed several Christmases as a recuperating hospital for Union soldiers. After the war it was sold for taxes, as were many beautiful old South Carolina homes. It went through various incarnations as boarding houses and inns, and was recently restored to its gracious antebellum splendor. At Christmas, the current proprietors of the inn keep the decorations simple, allowing the beauty of the house and gardens to take the spotlight.

Rhett House Inn, Beaufort

"Only to think this is Christmas Eve. Wonder what the good friends are all doing up in Chester County. But why wonder. No doubt they are, as we are, thinking about some friends. We, that is, the tenants of #6 Lincoln Row, have been churning our brains for the last few days in the vain hope of producing something extra for Christmas dinner. But with all our efforts, mental and physical, we have been unable to produce anything equal to half a pound of Chester County butter. A few of us tried hard to get [around] the picketts on a foraging expedition with the hope of getting a fresh turkey, but failed to get a pass. Some of the boys were so cruel this afternoon as to steal…three young alligators each about two feet long which we had confined in a tub of water. Guess we will have to make a 'Sardine Stew.'"

—HARRY KAUFFMAND

a Union Soldier stationed on Hilton Head Island, December 24, 1861.
(Courtesy of the South Caroliniana Library Archives, University of South Carolina.)

When I grew up in Jenkinsville there were three stores and a post office. Now there are only two stores, but we still have the post office. We owe our thanks to our long-time postmistress, Katherine Meadows, for keeping it in town. She sold stamps to friends and relatives all across the country, thus having enough sales volume—especially at Christmastime—to keep the post office in Jenkinsville.

—JUDY C. MILLINAX, *formerly of Jenkinsville*

Our favorite tradition is reading THE NIGHT BEFORE CHRISTMAS *to our children on Christmas Eve before going to bed. Our oldest child is now 26 years old and the youngest 17. This has been a family tradition for 26 years.*

—JUDY L. LOWDER, *Columbia*

JOGGLING BOARD

Tradition has it that many marriages between fine South Carolina families had their beginnings on the joggling board, an interesting wooden structure found in many of the state's yards. Used almost like a balance beam or trampoline by younger children, courting couples were said to have sat on it, at first far apart, but ultimately together as the board bounced them both toward the sagging center.

Joggling board, Hopsewee Plantation, Georgetown

We love the children's Christmas Eve service at our church, the First Presbyterian in Greenville. The service includes a songfest, children's sermon, the Christmas message, and it closes with a live nativity scene.

—ALICE BARRON STEWART
Greenville

We gather together on Christmas Eve and the men in the family take turns telling the Christmas story, asking questions of the children as they read.

—BETTY F. DENT
Columbia

Above: Shiloh Methodist Church, 210 years old, near Gramling;
Right: First Baptist Church, Campobello

Every year we try to include others in our holiday celebrations. One year we had a party for some men at the rescue mission. Another year we had a party for internationals who were here in Greenville over the holidays. We often have white elephant exchanges at these parties, which is always a lot of fun. This past year for some reason we didn't have a party, but on December 24 we took a lonely old woman to the children's service at church and then invited her to our home for dinner. These small attempts to share and bring joy to others are important for us and our children.

—CLARE FRIST, Greenville

Left: "The First Christmas," Gramling United Methodist Church

On Christmas Eve, the grand-children who live near us come to our house for a birthday party for Jesus. We have a formal dinner in the dining room, with my husband and me serving. Each child, the oldest is twelve and the youngest is four, takes a turn sitting at the head of the table, playing host. After dinner my husband reads them the Christmas story from the Bible and talks to them about the true meaning of Christmas.

—MR. AND MRS.
B. PALMER MCARTHUR
Columbia

Handmade Chrismon

Symme's Chapel at "A Pretty Place," a favorite overlook in the mountains

The Chrismon Tree of Faith

Many South Carolina churches follow a lovely old Christian tradition when they decorate their sanctuaries for the holidays. Gold and white ornaments called Chrismons are hung on the tree along with small lights. Usually handcrafted by members of the congregation, each Chrismon symbolizes an aspect of the Christian faith. Some are made in the shapes of crosses or crowns; others are angels, stars, or flowers, such as dogwoods or lilies; and there are also Greek and Latin letters that have special significance throughout Christendom. The women of the First United Methodist Church in Cheraw have been adding to their handmade collection of Chrismons for years, and nearly 200 of the delicate ornaments adorn the massive cedar tree in their 146-year-old church. For them, the Chrismons are a radiant statement of their faith.

STARS AND ANGELS DANCE IN FLIGHT

by Doug Kracht, Columbia

Every year at Christmastime, our family selects a specific theme around which we center our celebrations. In 1996 the theme came from a poem from *Hodie: A Christmas Cantata* by Ralph Vaughn Williams.

After hearing the poem I began looking for Christmassy objects that looked like stars and angels dancing in flight. Unable to find anything satisfactory, I began perusing shelves and counters of Christmas cards looking to illustrate the poem's last line, "Such a light such dark did span." If I hadn't been looking for it, I would not have given it a second glance. The card was blue, ninety percent night sky with a large bright star at the top. The star's white ray shoots down through an atmosphere of swirling pale blue angels and stars to a Judean village below, causing a small incandescent glow at a scarcely distinguishable spot center stage. It was not a complicated concept. I bought it and 49 identical others.

Deciding that the image suffered because of its small scale, I took the card to the local photocopy store for an 11 x 17-inch enlargement to use as a poster to decorate our home for Christmas. The store was about to have its grand opening, so the staff had been trained but was still inexperienced in handling the special request. After a great deal of fussing over the copy machine, the first copy came out to the literal gasp—and relief—of the four employees. I was so pleased at their success that, throwing any thoughts of budget to the wind, I immediately ordered ten more copies, not wanting to lose the perfect electronic combination.

So these beautiful blue declarations of the real meaning of Christmas came rolling out to the silent stares of that secular establishment. As I was paying for them, the manager came up and asked me to show the employees at the front what the others at the back had seen. I agreed on the condition that I could also quote the poem. I spread the copies out before the gathering crowd of clerks as I began, "Promise fills the sky with light...."

What followed in the hush that hollowed the commercial music playing in the background was the voice of one of the clerks who said, "Oh, that makes me want to cry." I think it was at that moment that Christmas was really Christmas for me that year. With the light of the star shining on the birth of Jesus and angels dancing in the sky, the soft incandescence of Christmas filled my soul.

> Promise fills the sky with light,
> Stars and angels dance in flight;
> Joy of heaven shall now unbind
> Chains of evil from mankind,
> Love and joy their power shall break,
> And for a newborn prince's sake;
> Never since the world began
> Such a light such dark did span.
> —*from* HODIE: A CHRISTMAS CANTATA

We attend the candlelight service at our church every Christmas Eve. The church is filled with people, the lights are dim, and the music is beautiful. This past year our five-year-old daughter, Caroline, assisted with the lighting of the candles. Her little face just glowed and she looked like an angel!

—CAROL TIMANUS
Fountain Inn

Decorations at the South Carolina Historic Society's annual open house, Charleston

Old Sheldon Church ruins, near Beaufort, are all that remain of Prince William's Parish Church (built in 1754), burned first by the British and later by Union troops

On the wall of the Old Brick Church in Jenkinsville is a note from Sherman's troops apologizing to the congregation for "defacing the house of the Lord."

—JUDY C. MILLINAX
formerly of Jenkinsville

One of the finest traditions in Florence at Christmastime is the candlelight service on Christmas Eve at First Baptist Church. The service is simple but profound. Church members and non-members alike always look forward to this annual event. The tradition is made more meaningful as the sanctuary is decorated with poinsettias.

—JIMMIE E. HARLEY, Pastor, First Baptist Church, Florence

Mountain Hill Church, Glassy Mountain

Mary Had a Baby

Ma-ry had a Ba-by, Aye, Lord, Ma-ry had a Ba-by, Aye, my Lord,

Quiet (♩ = 60) smooth

Continue without pause

Ma-ry had a Ba-by, Aye, Lord, The peo-ple keep a-com-ing and the train done gone.

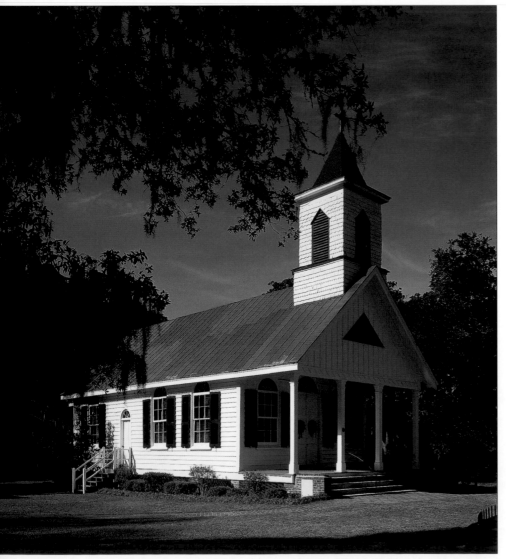

Trinity Episcopal Church, Edisto Island

2. Down in a valley.

3. What did she name Him?

4. Named Him Jesus.

5. Where was He born?

6. Born in a stable.

7. Where did she lay Him?

8. Laid Him in a manger.

9. Who came to see Him?

10. Shepards came to see Him.

11. Wise men brought
    Him presents.

12. King Herrod tried to
    find Him.

13. They went away to Egypt.

14. Mary rode the donkey.

15. Joseph walked beside them.

16. Angels watching over.

We attend the candlelight service on Christmas Eve and afterward have a birthday cake for Jesus. When our children were small, they would act out a skit. Now that they are grown, I really miss that part of our Christmas tradition. I'm hoping it will be renewed when we have grandchildren.

—REBECCA CHASON
Ballentine

We always place an Advent wreath on the dining room table and look forward with joy to lighting a candle each Sunday in December. We finally light the one in the center, reminding us of the birth of our precious Lord and Savior, Jesus Christ.

—MRS. JOHN F. HOOKER, JR., *Columbia*

A country church seen through live oaks, McClellanville

The Museum of Sacred Art

"Every good gift and every perfect gift is from above, and cometh down from the Father of lights," (James 1:17). So begins the self-guided tour of the Museum of Sacred Art at Bob Jones University in Greenville. Twenty-seven galleries display the works of the great masters: Botticelli, Titian, Rembrandt, Rubens, Van Dyck, and Murillo, to name but a few. This collection of Italian, Dutch, and Spanish paintings dates from 1590 to 1750 and is considered one of the finest assemblages of sacred art in the United States. The museum's display of more than 400 paintings has been praised by art critics the world over, particularly for its excellent collection of baroque painting.

Many of these works of art depict the story of Christmas, portraying the Annunciation, the birth of Christ, Mary and Joseph, and the shepherds and Magi. For the curators of the museum, theirs is a labor of love with a mission: to show the world that the birth of Jesus Christ put into motion a series of events that would change the course of history and dramatically change the lives of people touched by His teachings. During the Christmas season attendance at the Museum of Sacred Art increases as people are moved to view the Advent of Christ through the eyes of the great masters. The museum is open year-round Tuesday through Sunday from 2 to 5 P.M., and is closed December 20 to 25 and January 1.

"Adoration of the Magi" by Johann Broeckhorst, Flemish, 1605–1668

Every Christmas Eve our family gathers together and we pass the Bible around as each person reads part of the Christmas story. Christmas is an especially meaningful time for us because my husband is a pastor.

—VICKI LOUGHNER
Old 96

Throughout the Christmas season we focus on the reason for the holiday—the birth of Jesus. We celebrate the four weeks of Advent with candles, and we string many minilights throughout the house, because Christ is the Light of the World.

—ANN CLARKE
Columbia

"The Annunciation" by Il Cavaliere D'Arpino (Giuseppe Cesari), Roman, 1568–1640

Hanukkah

On the evening of the 25th day of Kislev, in the Hebrew lunar calendar, the South Carolina Jewish community begins one of the most joyous celebrations of the year—Hanukkah. The dates of the festival vary each year; it can be as early as November 28 and as late as December 24. Also known as the Festival of Lights, Hanukkah was first celebrated more than a hundred years before the birth of Christ, but because it falls around the same time of year, both Jews and Christians celebrate festively during the month of December. Hanukkah lasts for eights days, each night commemorated by lighting a candle on the Menorah. The burning candles signify a miraculous event in Hebrew history.

In 165 B.C. Judah Maccabee, his brother, and their small army defeated the powerful Syrian tyrant Antiochus. With great joy the Hebrew people cleansed their temple of the hated idols left behind by the Syrians. They could find only one small cruse of consecrated oil to rededicate the temple to God. It was not nearly enough. In faith, they lit the oil anyway, and to their great amazement it burned for eight days and nights, enough to last until more oil could be made.

Hanukkah celebrations in South Carolina center around family and friends. In Greenville, Dan and Elizabeth Einstein use a Menorah that has been in Dan's family for many years. Their whole family joins together to celebrate—grandparents, aunts, uncles, and, of course, the children. One of the favorite pastimes of their young sons is playing "dreidel" with their grandfather and cousins.

The dreidel is a simple, four-sided top inscribed with the Hebrew words "a miracle happened there." One child at a time spins the top, and, depending which side is showing when it stops spinning, the player will either win the "geld"— gold in the form of foil-wrapped chocolate coins—or forfeit some that he has already won. On each of the eight nights of Hanukkah, after the blessing and the lighting of the Menorah, the children are each given one small gift. The Einstein's often include imaginative ones, such as a coupon to stay up late. On the last night of Hanukkah, each child receives a special present.

Hanukkah is a time of visiting, high spirits, and, of course, food. Some traditional Hanukkah foods include challah (a type of bread) and homemade latkes (potato pancakes), which are served with applesauce and sour cream. Food and music, friends and neighbors, love and laughter—Hanukkah is a joyful occasion that brings the family together to celebrate a miracle that took place more than two thousand years ago.

A Hanukkah feast at the Einsteins' home

POTATO LATKES

6 cups grated potatoes (about 3 medium-large potatoes)

1 medium onion, grated

3 eggs, beaten

3 tablespoons all-purpose flour

2 teaspoons salt

Ground black pepper to taste

Olive oil for cooking

Place grated potatoes on paper towels and squeeze out as much moisture as possible. Place in a large bowl, add all other ingredients, except oil, and mix together. You may need to add a little more flour if mixture becomes too watery.

Heat ¼ inch of oil in a skillet on medium-high heat. Form potato mixture into 3-inch diameter patties, pressed as thin as possible. Brown on each side. Drain on brown paper grocery bags to remove as much oil as possible. Latkes are best if served immediately. However, if you need to hold them for serving, keep them warn in the oven. Serve with applesauce or sour cream.

Makes approximately 18 latkes

—ELIZABETH EINSTEIN, Greenville

Native American Christmas

When Chief Gilbert Blue of the Catawba nation tells his children and grandchildren about Christmas, he recites to them the timeless story of the birth of Christ—part of the spiritual heritage of his family, which converted to the Mormon faith. But this is only part of his spiritual heritage. As an American Indian he also sees Christmas as a time to remind his family about the many natural things God has created. "I tell them to remember how important the grass and trees and water are to our lives, and encourage them to be respectful of God's creation," says Chief Blue. "I don't want them to lose sight of these things."

Originally Siouan, ancestors of the Catawba migrated to South Carolina from the north, most likely Canada, and settled along the Catawba River. The Catawba (which means "people of the river") are the only federally recognized American Indian tribe in South Carolina, although small groups of other tribes also live here. The Catawba still maintain strong spiritual ties to the earth and carry on the tribal traditions that have

survived the years. Like other Indian peoples, most of the Catawba have adopted Christianity, often mingling Native American ways with traditional Christmas celebrations.

"When I was a boy we often used hides of animals to wrap our gifts," says Chief Blue. "We didn't have money to buy anything from a store or a catalog, so we used the things that God had created—things from the earth. We would be allowed to go into the orchards that surrounded the reservation to pick apples, which we piled up into the shape of a Christmas tree."

Pottery making is a Catawba tradition recognized worldwide for its beauty and simplicity in design. Using the same methods as their ancestors have for more than 500 years, Catawba women fashion handmade pottery using the coil method. First wrapping coils of clay around a mold—some molds have been handed down from mother to daughter for centuries—the potter then scrapes the clay to eliminate the coil lines and rubs it with a flat river rock to smooth the surface. She then allows the piece to dry. When it is dried and ready to fire, the piece is placed in a pit of hot coals, and wood is continually added to the pit until the firing is complete. The colors of the pottery are determined by the type of wood used in the firing process: ash and hickory create an orange-gray finish; pine a gray or black; and oak light yellow with gray color.

"When I was a boy our favorite food at Christmas was corn, still in the shuck, which we steamed in a pit. And we especially enjoyed deer stew."

—CHIEF GILBERT BLUE
Rock Hill

Kwanzaa

The African-American celebration of Kwanzaa encompasses the seven days from December 26 to January 1. Kwanzaa, meaning "first" in Swahili, was established in 1965 and is a uniquely American holiday. It is a time of unity when families and friends gather to celebrate their common heritage. Through music, dancing, arts and crafts, storytelling, prayer, and feasting, the African-American community joins in festively celebrating the season in their own unique way. Central to the symbolism of Kwanzaa is the kinara, which holds seven candles, each one signifying one of the seven principles of the African harvest. Each day one of the candles is lit, emphasizing such principles as self-determination, responsibility, and faith.

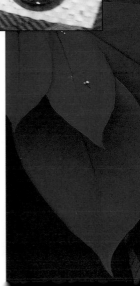

A Kwanzaa table with the kinara as centerpiece

PRINCIPLES OF KWANZAA

1. **UMOJA** (Unity)
2. **KUJICHAGULIA** (Self-determination)
3. **UJIMA** (Collective Work and Responsibility)
4. **UJAMMA** (Cooperative Economics)
5. **NIA** (Purpose)
6. **KUUMBA** (Creativity)
7. **IMANI** (Faith)

Being a native of Pawleys Island, I never felt Christmas
was like a Currier and Ives' painting. Short sleeves were
the better choice than heavy sweaters. Skis that floated
over water proved more practical than those that could
soar over snow. Yes, chestnuts did roast over open
fires, but those were bonfires on the beach, under the
stars, surrounded by family in shorts and T-shirts. The
warmth in the air always matched the warmth of the
Christmas season.

—**Tara McClary**
Pawleys Island and Columbia

*We have a large family and can't always be together
at Christmas. But we are only a phone call away.*

—**Mrs. Teresa Kleeblatt**
Fountain Inn

"It was hard to tear away from the many joys and
comforts with you all. We all went away feeling this was
the best Christmas we have ever had up to this time."

—**Mrs. E. W. Dabbs**
*in a letter to her daughter, Jessie, December 29, 1930.
(From the Dabbs Collection, courtesy of the South
Caroliniana Library, University of South Carolina.)*

Dawn, Edisto Beach

CHRISTMAS FOR NINE
by Dr. Thalia J. Coleman, formerly of Lake View

*M*ost of the people in my hometown of Lake View were very poor. Times were not easy for an African-American family with seven children living on a farm. Even though I had only two dresses as a child, my mother washed one out each night so I could go to school every day in a clean dress. We were poor, but we always had enough to eat. And absolutely the most wonderful part of Christmas was the food.

Preparations started about three days before Christmas. There was always a whole ham taken from the smokehouse and there was always a baked hen. Sometimes we had a possum or a coon. You have never tasted anything so good as our homemade cornbread stuffing. Everything was homemade, and most of it was from our own yard and fields. The best part was the pies and cakes—always six or seven kinds of cakes and about five kinds of pies, although there were more sweet potato pies than anything else.

The feasting started early Christmas morning and continued for at least two days, eating and drinking as much as we could possibly hold. Often people would drop by each others' homes and eat a "mouthful" of some dish they hadn't prepared at their own home. During the holidays you would never have thought us poor. We had so much food, I don't think even the Rockefellers could have eaten better. Nor do I think they could have been happier than our rural South Carolina family at Christmas.

SOUTHERN STYLE COLLARD GREENS WITH SMOKED TURKEY WINGS

1 pound smoked turkey wings
2 bundles collard greens
¼ cup white vinegar or cider vinegar
1 teaspoon sugar

1½ teaspoons salt
½ teaspoon black pepper
¼ teaspoon crushed red pepper
¼ teaspoon baking powder

Cover turkey wings with water in stock pot and cook over medium-high heat until tender. Wash greens thoroughly; strip off stems and remove all bad leaves. Add greens to turkey wings and cook for 1 hour on low heat. Add remaining ingredients and cook another 30 minutes on low heat. Serve hot.

Makes 10 servings

—**CHEF ANDRÈ,** *Beaufort, prepared for The Rhett House Inn*

VANGIE'S OYSTER STEW

2 pints fresh oysters, shucked
½ cup butter (1 stick)
2 14-ounce cans evaporated milk

2 quarts whole milk
Salt and pepper to taste

In a stew pot, sauté oysters in butter. Slowly add both milks and bring to boil. Add salt and pepper and let simmer for about ½ hour. One of our grandsons sautés chopped onions and garlic along with the oysters.

Serves 12–15   —**VANGY MABRY,** *Rock Hill*

Lowcountry Christmas dinner presented at the Rhett House Inn by Chef Andrè, Beaufort

ROASTED TOM TURKEY WITH FRESH HERBS AND VEGETABLES

1 10- to 12-pound young fresh Tom turkey
1 medium onion, quartered
2 carrots, cut in half

2 celery stalks, cut in half
2–4 sprigs of thyme
2–4 sprigs of oregano

Preheat oven to 350° F.

Wash turkey thoroughly with water. Place in an open roasting pan, breast side up, and stuff with vegetables and herbs. Bake turkey for 3½ to 4 hours, basting regularly. When skin is an even golden brown, cover the turkey with an aluminum foil tent so that the bird does not burn on the outside or dry out inside. To check for doneness, move the leg joint up and down. It should give readily or break. When done cooking, remove the vegetables and use around the turkey as a garnish. Let stand for at least 10 minutes before slicing.

Serves 10–12

—CHEF ANDRÈ, *Beaufort, prepared for The Rhett House Inn*

ROAST STUFFED LOIN OF PORK WITH MIXED FRUIT AND NUT STUFFING

1 4- to 5-pound boneless pork loin
½ cup fresh basil pesto
2 tablespoons Italian seasoned bread crumbs
6 thin slices prosciutto ham
1 8-ounce package Berry Good brand dried fruit mix (cranberries, blueberries, cherries, pineapple, raisins, almonds, walnuts)
½ cup applesauce

1 tablespoon fresh chopped garlic, mixed in a little oil (prepared in advance and refrigerated)
1 tablespoon kosher salt
1 tablespoon black pepper, coarse ground
4 sprigs fresh rosemary
1 cup apple juice
Potatoes and onions as desired

Preheat oven to 450° F.

Trim and butterfly pork loin. Spread pesto evenly over inside cavity of meat (reserving 1 tablespoon) and sprinkle lightly with bread crumbs. Arrange prosciutto over pesto mixture and top with reserved pesto.

Mix dried fruits with applesauce and spoon on top of prosciutto. Carefully roll up meat, keeping cut seam on the bottom. Tie roast with butcher's twine.

Heat roasting pan on top of stove and sear meat until evenly browned on all sides. Rub with garlic, season with salt and pepper, top with fresh rosemary. Add apple juice to pan and potatoes and onions if desired.

Place in oven for 1 hour and 15 minutes, or until an internal temperature of 150° F on meat thermometer. Let rest for 10 to 15 minutes before serving.

Makes 10–12 servings

—CHEF BRUCE A. SACINO, *The Governor's Mansion, Columbia*

SHRIMP GUMBO

½ pound bacon, chopped
½ pound smoked ham
½ pound smoked sausage, chopped
1 medium onion, chopped
½ red bell pepper, chopped
½ green bell pepper, chopped
All-purpose flour, sifted
2 quarts chicken stock
½ pound okra, trimmed and sliced
1 12-ounce can diced tomatoes, drained
½ of a 6-ounce can of tomato paste

2 cloves garlic, chopped finely
1 teaspoon salt
1 teaspoon ground thyme
½ teaspoon ground chili powder
½ teaspoon ground cumin
¼ teaspoon white pepper
¼ teaspoon ground curry powder
⅛ teaspoon cayenne pepper
1 pound medium shrimp
  (approximately 25), raw but
  peeled and deveined

In large sauce pan, combine bacon, ham, sausage, onion, red and green peppers, and cook over medium-high heat until onions are translucent. Sprinkle a little flour over the meat and vegetable mixture, and stir until a pasta-like consistency. Cook for 5 minutes more.

In a large stock pot, combine chicken stock, okra, tomatoes, tomato paste and seasonings. Cook on medium-high heat 7 to 10 minutes, until okra is tender. Slowly add meat-paste mixture to stock pot. Stirring constantly, cook for 10 to 15 minutes on low heat. Add shrimp 3 to 5 minutes before heating is complete.

Serve hot over white steamed rice.

Serves 10

—**CHEF ANDRÈ**, *Beaufort, prepared for The Rhett House Inn*

We have a family gathering on Christmas Eve and eat fried oysters and oyster stew. My mother, Vangie W. Mabry, age 93, remembers this as her family tradition way back to when she was a little girl. The ladies prepare the meal while the men in the family enjoy a raw oyster cocktail on a saltine cracker with hot sauce and chopped onions.

—**NORMA SORGEE**
Rock Hill

SEAFOOD JAMBALAYA

½ pound bacon, chopped
1 pound long-grain rice
1 medium onion, chopped
3 cloves garlic, chopped
3 cups chicken stock
1 2-ounce can tomato paste
1 teaspoon Old Bay seasoning
¼ teaspoon white pepper
¼ teaspoon chili pepper

¼ teaspoon ground cumin
⅛ teaspoon cayenne pepper
1–2 bay leaves
½ pound shucked oysters
½ pound lump crab meat
1 pound medium shrimp
  (approximately 25), raw but
  peeled and deveined
¼ pound littleneck clams

In a large stock pot, cook bacon in its own fat until tender. Add rice, onion and garlic to the pan and cook until onions are translucent and rice slightly brown.

Add chicken stock, tomato paste, seasonings and bay leaves and cook on medium heat for 10 minutes. Add seafood and cook, covered, for 25 to 30 minutes in the oven at 350° F or until rice is tender, and clams pop open.

Makes 12 to 14 servings

—**CHEF ANDRÈ**, *Beaufort, prepared for The Rhett House Inn*

We don't have the same meal every Christmas, as many people do. For us each year is different. This year I decided I didn't want turkey—Thanksgiving was enough—so we had ham on Christmas Eve and steak for Christmas dinner.

—**CLARE FRIST**
Greenville

AN OLD COUNTRY CHRISTMAS
by Dr. Carol Toris, Charleston

In my family, Christmas Eve is a day of fasting and abstinence, meaning only one meatless meal is eaten that day. This tradition was brought over by my Slovak and Lithuanian grandparents. This special ceremonial meal marks the preparation for the Christmas holiday for Catholics in Slovakia, Poland, and Lithuania. Although the particular foods offered at this meal vary from family to family, certain traditions are common, such as there are thirteen "courses," representing Christ and His Apostles. My mother counted everything, including the coffee and cake for dessert, as separate courses!

A place is set at the table for absent family members, including those who have passed away. In the old days, it was common to invite a destitute person to occupy this place of honor. When I was growing up, we called this setting the "poor plate," and we were expected to contribute to it from our own plates. You were supposed to give whatever foods were your favorites, and someone was expected to contribute from each course.

The meal always began with a blessing of holy water from the head of the household, a prayer, and a toast (my family preferred Manischewicz blackberry wine). Oplatky, or unleavened bread (like the kind used for communion hosts), was always the first course. This bread was given out by the churches to the parishioners for the occasion. It came in small squares, about three inches by five inches, and was embossed with a Christmas scene. Since there are no Slovak churches here in South Carolina, I must now buy my oplatky from a bakery in New York. My favorite part of the meal was the oplatky course, which symbolized the bitter and the sweet events of the coming year. The main course was smoked fish. My family always had smoked whiting, but that's not available here in South Carolina either, so I usually substitute smoked whitefish or even smoked salmon. Another "course" would consist of cracking open a walnut. If you got a rotten one, your number was up that year!

Once a meal began, no one could get up from the table except the "woman of the house," who served each course separately and only after the previous one was completed. After the meal, we usually opened our gifts. Santa came on Christmas Eve since the next day, Christmas, was a religious holiday. If we could stay up long enough, we'd go to midnight mass.

In 43 years I've never missed a traditional Christmas Eve meal. It always serves to bring me closer to my ancestors, to my family, and to the real meaning of Christmas.

FROGMORE STEW

2 pounds smoked sausage,
  cut into 2-inch lengths
4 tablespoons Old Bay seasoning
  or equivalent

1 medium onion, chopped
5 ears corn, halved
3 pounds raw shrimp, shelled and deveined

Bring approximately 2 gallons of water to a boil in a large pot. Add sausage, onion and seasoning, and return to a boil. Add corn and return to boil. Continue boiling until corn is done, about 15 minutes. Add shrimp, stirring often, until they just turn pink, about 4 minutes. Do not overcook shrimp.

Drain water and ladle stew onto a table covered with newspaper for easy cleanup. Serve with butter or cocktail sauce, and eat with your fingers and use paper towels like the people in Frogmore do. Goes down well with cold beer. Mmmmm, good!

Serves approximately 10. Add more of everything to the water if your guests haven't eaten in a week.

—Reprinted with permission from Beautiful Beaufort by the Sea, Coastal Villages Press, Beaufort

At Christmas we always celebrated with a huge dinner, for we had extended family next door—three houses!

—ANN ELLIS KEETER
Columbia

OYSTER CORNBREAD DRESSING

1 9 x 9 pan cornbread, coarsely broken
½ loaf day-old bread, chopped or crumbled
1 tablespoon ground sage
1 teaspoon poultry seasoning
¼ teaspoon ground thyme
1 teaspoon salt

¼ teaspoon black pepper
3 tablespoons butter
1 medium onion, chopped fine
2 stalks celery, chopped fine
1 cup soup stock (chicken broth or cubes)
8 ounces fresh oysters, shucked

Preheat oven to 350° F.

Combine cornbread, day-old bread, sage, poultry seasoning, thyme, and salt and pepper in large mixing bowl. Melt butter in pan and sauté onions and celery over medium-high heat until tender. Add to bread mixture.

Heat soup stock and add to bread mixture, tossing slightly to incorporate but not to over-mix. Add oysters and toss again.

Place dressing in well-greased pan and bake for 30 to 45 minutes. Serve hot or use for stuffing.

Makes 20 servings   **—CHEF ANDRÈ,** *Beaufort, prepared for The Rhett House Inn*

Our baked Christmas ham is basted with Coca-Cola. This was first done at my aunt's house and has continued as a tradition in our home. The soda gives the ham a wonderful, sweet taste.

—KEVIN PARKER
Union

CRANBERRY SAUCE

1 pound fresh cranberries
1 cup sugar

1 stick cinnamon (or 1 teaspoon ground)
¼ cup cornstarch

Place cranberries in stock pot and cover with water. Reserve ¼ cup of liquid from pot and cool. Add sugar and cinnamon, and cook on medium-high heat until cranberries bleed and soften.

Combine cornstarch with the ¼ cup of liquid from the stock pot and stir until smooth. When this has cooled slightly, return it to stock pot. Stir cranberry mixture until smooth and thickened. Remove cinnamon stick. Serve hot or cold.

Makes 25 servings   **—CHEF ANDRÈ,** *Beaufort, prepared for The Rhett House Inn*

GREEN BEAN CASSEROLE

2 9-ounce packages frozen
  French-style green beans
4 tablespoons butter
1 medium onion, sliced
1 4-ounce can mushrooms,
  stems and pieces
1 tablespoon flour
1 cup milk

⅓ cup New York sharp cheddar cheese,
  grated
½ of an 8-ounce can water chestnuts,
  chopped
1 tablespoon Worcestershire sauce
½ teaspoon soy sauce
Salt and pepper to taste
Slivered, toasted almonds

Preheat oven to 375° F.

Cook beans according to package directions. In large pan, melt butter and sauté onion and mushrooms. Add flour, milk and cheese and let thicken.

Add beans, water chestnuts, Worcestershire and soy sauce, and salt and pepper. Mix well and put in glass casserole. Bake 15 minutes. Garnish with slivered, toasted almonds.

Serves 12–15   —**ALICE BARRON STEWART,** *Greenville*

WALDORF SALAD WITH ROASTED PECANS AND FENNEL SEEDS

1 tablespoon butter
1 cup pecan halves
3 tablespoons mayonnaise
2 tablespoons fennel seeds
1 teaspoon sugar

1 teaspoon lemon juice
½ teaspoon salt
¼ teaspoon white pepper
½ head cabbage, shredded
1 green apple, cored, peeled and diced

Preheat oven to 350° F.

Melt butter and pour over pecans. Roast for 10 minutes in oven. Let stand for later use. In a large bowl, combine mayonnaise, fennel seeds, sugar, lemon juice, and salt and pepper to make dressing. Toss with cabbage and apples and chill. Mix in pecans right before serving.

Serves 8–10   —**CHEF ANDRÈ,** *Beaufort, prepared for The Rhett House Inn*

GREEN BEANS, YODER STYLE

2 9-ounce packages frozen green beans
2 tablespoons margarine
2 tablespoons flour
1 cup sour cream
1 tablespoon grated onion

1 teaspoon sugar
1 teaspoon each salt and pepper
½ pound Swiss cheese, grated
2 cups corn flakes, crushed
3 tablespoons margarine, cut up

Preheat oven to 375° F.

Cook green beans according to package directions and place in greased casserole. Melt 2 tablespoons margarine and stir in flour. Add sour cream, onion, sugar and salt and pepper. Fold sauce into beans and cover with cheese. Mix corn flakes with remaining margarine and spread on top. Bake for 30 minutes.

Serves 10–12   —**HELEN YODER,** *Greenville*

My husband and I grew up in a small, rural farming community in Hampton County. Estill was a wonderful town and still is. My husband and his three brothers all moved away, but their roots call them back home to the Lowcountry every Christmas. The land, the good memories, and Mersty's fried chicken and biscuits draw us back again and again. Hunting is also part of the season, and the holidays always bring to mind memories of muddy boots, pick-up trucks, shotguns, and venison and grits.

—**POLLY BOWERS**
Columbia, formerly of Estill

AUNT PAULINE'S CRANBERRY SALAD

2 cups fresh cranberries

1 whole unpeeled naval orange,
  cut in wedges or slices

1 cup sugar

1 8-ounce can crushed pineapple,
  drained (reserve juice)

1 small package (3-ounce size)
  raspberry Jell-O

1 tablespoon plain Knox gelatin

1 cup diced celery

½ cup chopped pecans or walnuts

Run the cranberries and orange through food processor until finely chopped.
Add sugar and pineapple. Stir and set aside.

In a medium bowl, make the raspberry Jell-O according to package directions.
Soften plain gelatin in reserved pineapple juice and add to Jell-O. Set aside to firm slightly.
When the Jell-O is partially set, add fruit mixture, celery and nuts, and mix well. Pour the
mixture into a mold sprayed with Pam and refrigerate until congealed. Unmold the salad
and garnish with parsley or a dab of mayonnaise. This salad can be made 2 to 3 days ahead.

Serves 8–12

—**ANN L. CLARKE,** *Columbia*

NATURAL GRAVY

3 tablespoons butter

1 tablespoon all-purpose flour

4 tablespoons stock (from meat drippings)

¼ cup water

¼ teaspoon salt

⅛ teaspoon white pepper

In a sauce pan, melt butter slowly over medium-low heat. Add flour and stir until
smooth. Cook for 7 minutes. Combine stock and water together, and add to sauce pan.
Stir until smooth, and season with salt and pepper.

Serves 8 people

—**CHEF ANDRÈ,** *Beaufort, prepared for The Rhett House Inn*

BUTTERNUT SQUASH

1 large butternut squash

4 tablespoons margarine, cut up

2 eggs, beaten

½ cup brown sugar

½ cup milk

½ teaspoon vanilla

Dash nutmeg

Preheat oven to 350° F.

Cut squash in half and bake for 30 minutes, or until soft, in a shallow pan with ½ inch
of water. Scoop pulp from skins, mash and then measure out 1½ cups of cooked squash.
Add margarine to squash and stir until melted. Add all other ingredients and mix well.

Bake for approximately 30 to 40 minutes in square 9 x 9 glass pan.

Serves 10–12

—**JENNIFER PRINCE,** *Irmo*

John Rutledge House

Just in time for Christmas of 1763, distinguished statesman John Rutledge and his bride, Elizabeth Grimke, moved into their new home in the center of Charles Town. The Rutledges loved to entertain, and the ballroom of their elegant home provided the perfect setting. Their Christmas party that year was the highlight of the social season.

One of the signers of the U.S. Constitution, John Rutledge also wrote much of the first draft of the document, which he composed in the library of his stately home. George Washington breakfasted at the Rutledge home in 1771. While Washington and Rutledge were good friends, Washington's diary entry for that date mentions only his hostess, Mrs. Rutledge. But is it likely that matters of historical importance were discussed as well.

Many official functions took place in the house at 116 Broad Street, and Rutledge's numerous friends, many of them politicians and important statesmen, frequented the gracious antebellum mansion. It was here that Rutledge wrote the state constitution of South Carolina.

John Rutledge House Inn, Charleston

During his illustrious career, Rutledge, a distinguished lawyer and judge, served as president of the Republic of South Carolina during the American Revolution, chairman of the South Carolina delegation to the Constitutional Convention in Philadelphia in 1787, and as governor of South Carolina. Later in life he became chief justice of South Carolina and finally chief justice of the United States' Supreme Court.

The John Rutledge House is one of only fifteen homes still standing that belonged to the original 55 signers of the U.S. Constitution, and it is the only one now in use as an inn. Often called the most historic inn in America, the house has been completely refurbished, and guests are treated with the same graciousness today as when the Rutledges lived there. Charleston's famous she-crab soup has always been attributed to subsequent owner, Mayor Rhett, whose butler reportedly created the recipe.

The staff of the inn has started the delightful tradition of a Christmas progressive supper, which is held on two weekends in December. Guests assemble at the Kings Courtyard Inn for hors d'oeuvres, walk to Anson's restaurant for dinner, and finish at the John Rutledge House Inn for dessert in the ballroom, where John and Elizabeth first entertained their holiday guests more than 230 years ago.

Charleston's annual Christmas parade is on the first Sunday of December. Because the parade route goes down Broad Street right past the Rutledge House, we've chosen this day for our employee Christmas party. Staff members from all four of our inns, as well as guests at the Rutledge House, gather together to enjoy food, drinks, and fellowship—with the Christmas parade as the main entertainment.

—LINDA BISHOP, *John Rutledge House Inn, Charleston*

SHE-CRAB SOUP

5 tablespoons butter

½ cup finely chopped celery

⅔ teaspoon mace

¼ teaspoon white pepper

3½ cups milk

½ cup chicken stock

5 tablespoons all-purpose flour

Salt to taste

2 cups crab meat*

1 cup heavy cream

¼ cup Worcestershire sauce

3 tablespoons sherry

2 hard-boiled egg yolks, grated
  (optional)

Paprika *(optional)*

Heat butter in large sauce pan. Add celery, mace and white pepper. Cook over low heat until celery is almost transparent.

While celery is cooking, heat milk and chicken stock in small pan, just enough to make milk hot without boiling. When celery is done, add flour to make a roux. Do not brown, but heat enough to bubble for several minutes. Slowly add milk and chicken stock to roux, add salt for taste.

If using fresh crab meat, shred the meat then pick over well to remove any cartilage and shell. If using canned crab, drain juice from can, flake meat with fork and pick over well. Add crab meat, cream, Worcestershire sauce and sherry. Simmer for 30 minutes or until quite thick. As a garnish you can grate the hard-boiled egg yolks and sprinkle paprika on top. Serve hot.

*"She-crabs" are considered a delicacy because they are much tastier than "he-crabs." The orange-hued eggs of she-crabs give the soup extra flavor and color. The grated egg yolk as garnish imitates the crab eggs. She-crabs are difficult to find in many parts of the country so white crab meat may be substituted.

Makes 18–20 small bowls

—**JOHN RUTLEDGE HOUSE INN,** *Charleston*

*Charleston's progressive supper ends
with dessert in the Rutledge House Inn's ballroom*

SHRIMP AND GRITS

4 cups water

1 teaspoon salt

3 tablespoons butter

1 cup grits

½ cup cream

1 teaspoon seasoning salt

½ pound fresh, uncooked shrimp
  (heads and tails off)

½ cup sliced or diced celery

Salt and pepper to taste

Bring the 4 cups of water to a boil, add salt and 2 tablespoons of butter. Reduce heat to medium. Add grits, stirring constantly. Simmer for 45 minutes or more, adding more water if needed for proper consistency. (If you are not a Southerner, grits should have the consistency of a thick cream of wheat.) Add cream and heat gently.

Bring a large pot of water to a boil. Add seasoning salt and cook shrimp until pink.

Sauté celery in remaining tablespoon of butter. (You can also add minced garlic if you like.) Add shrimp to the celery and heat gently. Season with salt and pepper.

Serve the shrimp over grits, topping with a garnish of grated sharp Cheddar cheese.

Makes 10–12 large servings

—**JOHN RUTLEDGE HOUSE INN,** *Charleston*

Each December we don our favorite Christmas sweatshirts and devote a week to creating a truly magical holiday feeling. We drape the ironwork on the porches with fresh pine roping tied with red velvet bows. We hang fresh pine wreaths on the doors, and inside the bannister is adorned with a garland of burgundy velvet ribbons and bows. A fresh fruit arrangement decorates the ballroom mantle next to the twelve-foot tree, which sparkles with 300 ornaments and more than 2,000 lights.

—**STAFF OF THE JOHN
RUTLEDGE HOUSE INN**

Charleston

THE STORY OF JESSYE'S CAROL
(THIS CHRISTMASTIDE)
by Composer Don Fraser

On Christmas Eve 1985, I was invited, along with several other people, to dinner at the English country house of the great American singer Jessye Norman. The room where we were entertained was done beautifully, with a large tree covered in lovely decorations, gifts for the guests laid out beneath it, and candles everywhere.

After a sumptuous meal, Ms. Norman went to make coffee for her guests, one of whom was Jane McCulloch, the playwright and author. Around 11:30, while Ms. Norman was in the kitchen, I suggested to Jane that we write a carol as a thank you gift for our splendid evening. Jane said she didn't know where to begin writing a lyric, and I said, rather glibly, "Well, start with the wrapping paper."

"Oh! You mean like green and silver and red and gold?"

"Yea, that'll do," I added.

Jane went to the kitchen to get some paper towels to write on. I then set the words to music, and twenty minutes later it was done. At precisely midnight on Christmas Day we sang it through and presented the carol to Jessye. That is why it is called Jessye's Carol. The kitchen towel and the music, which I wrote on a sheet of paper from my filofax, are today framed and hanging in the kitchen—where else?

Winter sunrise, Caesars Head

This Christmastide

Composed and arranged by Donald Fraser
Words by Jane McCulloch
Adapted by Kenny Bullock

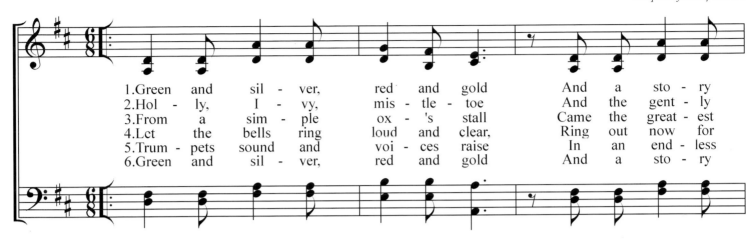

1. Green and sil - ver, red and gold And a sto - ry
2. Hol - ly, I - vy, mis - tle - toe And the gent - ly
3. From a sim - ple ox - 's stall Came the great - est
4. Let the bells ring loud and clear, Ring out now for
5. Trum - pets sound and voi - ces raise In an end - less
6. Green and sil - ver, red and gold And a sto - ry

born of old
fall - ing snow.
gift of all
all to hear
stream of praise,
born of old

1-5. Truth and love and hope a-bide, This
6. Peace and love and hope a-bide, This

Christ - mas - tide. This Christ - mas - tide.

Christ - mas - tide. This Christ - mas - tide.

Overleaf: Fog over the Sampit River, Georgetown

*Choral performance in front
of the courthouse, Newberry*

*Above: Charleston Community Band performs in the
King Street Square Christmas Festival, Charleston*

Left: Holiday bell choir, Fountain Inn

CHRISTMAS A WORLD AWAY
by Clebe McClary, Pawleys Island

My most memorable Christmas was, ironically, the first Christmas I didn't spend in South Carolina. It was Christmas 1967, and I was on Freedom Hill in Vietnam. My wife, Deanna, and I had been married earlier that year on Easter Sunday. Not only was it my first Christmas away from Carolina, it was my first Christmas as a married man and I was thousands of miles away from my lovely bride.

I was 1st Lt. McClary, in charge of a reconnaissance team in the jungles of Vietnam. We had been out on patrol for a good many days that lonely December, and when we reported back in, Colonel Stinmetz told us that Bob Hope was at Freedom Hill, near Da Nang. We didn't shave or even clean up. We just jumped in the back of a truck and headed off to celebrate Christmas with Bob Hope.

When we got to Freedom Hill, there must have been a half million Marines and soldiers packed into the outdoor amphitheater there in the mountains. Just hours earlier we had been using our telescopes and binoculars to scout out the enemy in the jungle, and now we used them to get a better view of Bob Hope and his show.

The comedy was corny, the songs were loud, and Raquel Welch or some other actress like that was there to add the dazzle. It was a great show and it helped take our minds off the real reason we were so far away from home at Christmastime. But what stays in my mind, almost 30 years later, was the sound of thousands, tens of thousands of Marines, in the middle of war-torn Vietnam, sitting on a hill singing "Silent Night." On the other side of Da Nang, planes were breaking the sound barrier, rockets were exploding in the distance, chaos and destruction went on all around us—but "silent night, holy night, all is calm, all is bright" is what we sang.

There was very little peace around us, but at that moment, half a world away from my Carolina home, I truly felt at peace. That is the joy of Christmas—whether you're surrounded by family and friends at the old homestead or sitting on a hill in the middle of a war, the Christ of Christmas can reach down and fill your heart with the peace that only He can give. No holiday since then has ever meant more than that Christmas with Bob Hope and thousands of Marines on Freedom Hill.

That was Clebe McClary's first and only Christmas in Vietnam. Less than three months later, he sat on another hill with his recon team, deep in the jungle, knowing that the enemy was waiting for an opportunity to attack. In the midnight clash that followed, he lost two men and suffered injuries that would keep him in the hospital for almost three years. His left eye and left arm were gone and he almost didn't make it home alive. Freedom Hill, the sight of that Bob Hope Christmas show, was later destroyed. Today Clebe is a motivational speaker, and he and Deanna have both written inspirational books about their experiences.

The annual "Christmas at the Lake" event, Aiken

Our favorite tradition is caroling in the neighborhood. Several families, children too, get together and sing outside people's homes. Then we go to a neighbor's for food and fellowship.

—MARY AUGUSTINE
Columbia

The Palmetto Mastersingers

What do a jeweler, a computer programmer, a golf pro, an ophthalmologist, and a massage therapist have in common? They and 95 other men come together to sing in the Palmetto Mastersingers. From all walks of life, and from throughout South Carolina, they are drawn together through their love of singing.

For fifteen years the Palmetto Mastersingers have raised their voices in song, performing at Carnegie Hall, the National Cathedral in Washington D.C., and even at The White House, where they were invited to sing during the 1995 Christmas season. Calling themselves "South Carolina's Musical Ambassadors to the World," the Mastersingers have performed internationally as well; during their 1997 European tour they sang the Solemn Mass at the Chair Altar in St. Peter's Basilica in Rome.

Back home in South Carolina, they often provide choral accompaniment for musical shows and symphony orchestras. To the delight of Columbia audiences, the Mastersingers perform a number of local concerts throughout the year, and for many people, the holiday season starts with the Palmetto Mastersingers' Christmas concert. This annual performance includes a mix of traditional and contemporary music. The Mastersingers have added "Betelehemu" to their repertoire, an African song that has become very popular in South Carolina. With the lyrics "Where was He born? In Bethlehem, city of wonder, praise be to Him!" it is a song rejoicing for the birth of Christ.

Members of the Palmetto Mastersingers, Columbia

Betelehemu
(Nigerian Christmas Song)

Via Olatunji
Arranged by Wendell Whalum
Adapted by Kenny Bullock

Yoruba dialect

Ni-bo la-bi Je - su, ni-bo la-be bi - i, ni-bo la-bi Je - su,

ni-bo la-be bi - i. Be-te-le-he - mu i-lu a-ra, ni-be la bi

Ba-ba o da-ju. Be-te-le-he-mu i-lu a-ra, Ni-be la-bi Ba-ba o da-ju

The Singing Christmas Tree

SHANDON BAPTIST CHURCH, COLUMBIA

A human Christmas tree standing 30 feet high, voices joined joyously in the songs of the season—this wondrous production is presented each year by the Shandon Baptist Church in Columbia. Over the past twelve years, more than 115,000 people have attended this holiday spectacle, and a good number return year after year. "The scripts and the music change each year," says director Dave Dupree. "but the message of Christmas is always the same. No matter what form the performance takes, it is always about the birth of Jesus, and His effect on mankind."

Scripts are written in the spring, the music is selected by June, and rehearsals start in September. Logistically, it's a huge undertaking. Four to five hundred people come together to put on the show. In addition to the 130-person "tree," there are another 36 who play in the orchestra, and about 250 more working as actors, directors, stage managers, lighting technicians, costumers, caterers, publicity people, ticket-sellers, ushers, parking attendants, and those who simply help out in any way they can. The Singing Tree has its own stage, special risers, coordinated robes and costumes, and special lighting effects. When the performances are over for the season, it takes an entire trailer to store all the equipment and material.

The Singing Christmas Tree

After the last riser has been folded and put away and the stage door locked, the hundreds of people who put the show together will know that the song that opens every performance has indeed come true—and that they have brought "Joy to the World."

At one performance of the singing tree, someone at the top of the tree became ill and was given a water bottle, which he accidentally kicked. He listened in embarrassment as it loudly bounced all the way down the risers to the bottom of the tree.

—DAVE DUPREE, *Columbia*

Summerall Chapel

THE CITADEL

"O come, O come Emmanuel…" intones the congregation of 1,200 worshipers gathered in the beautiful Summerall Chapel of Charleston's historic Citadel. On a Saturday evening in December, with candlelight warmly illuminating the aisles, the 56-voice Citadel Christmas Choir, accompanied by the Brass Ensemble, fills the vaulted chapel with music of the season. Interspersed with scripture passages, the choir leads the congregation through the Advent and birth of Christ, culminating with the jubilant "Joy to the World."

Summerall Chapel is a marvel of stained glass with 134 different windows. Depicting thirty events in the life of Christ, the Class Windows were presented by graduating classes of the military college. The spectacular Chancel Window is dedicated to the memory of Citadel men killed in action while defending their country. The stained glass windows, all crafted by the same company over a span of many years, combine with the chapel's lavish woodwork to create a sanctuary that is truly inspiring. The massive altar is supported by twelve buttresses, and the Appalachian Mountain white oak pews and paneled wainscoting are stained "cathedral brown."

Founded more than a century and a half ago by an act of the South Carolina legislature, The Citadel serves the dual purpose of educating young men and women and preparing them for the military. Historically it has been an all-male institution, and the early Corps of Cadets was responsible for guarding South Carolina's arsenal, which was located in the Spanish-Moorish building known as "the Citadel." When the military college was founded in 1842, it was named Citadel Academy, now called simply The Citadel. While maintaining strict military-style discipline, The Citadel is also a fully accredited liberal arts college.

Spiritual growth is encouraged and in keeping with this religious emphasis, the school maintains an interdenominational staff of ministers and counselors. Summerall Chapel remains open at all times for meditation and worship throughout the year. The loveliest service of all, however, is during the holiday season, when the chapel is aglow with candles and the sanctuary is filled with song. Summerall Chapel's Candlelight Service is a true Christmas gift to the people of Charleston.

Top: Trumpet fanfare at Summerall Chapel

Bottom: A Citadel cadet lights candles in the chapel

A Season of Sharing

Violins and canned food may seem an unlikely combination, but not at Christmas when the South Carolina Philharmonic presents its annual holiday performance—Concert Share.

The 70-member symphony orchestra joins with several choirs, theatre groups, a ballet company, and special guest artists in a community effort to provide food for those in need. Concertgoers cannot even buy a ticket to the event; a non-perishable food item is their admission price. The concert collects between 7,000 and 9,000 food items each year, which the Salvation Army then distributes. Backed by local sponsors and planned almost entirely by volunteer committees, Concert Share has been a holiday tradition in Columbia for more than 30 years—an outpouring of concern for others and a willingness to share that is in the true spirit of the season.

Top: Guest celebrities conduct at Concert Share
Bottom: The South Carolina Philharmonic joins with the Brookland Baptist Church Choir in performing "Go Tell it on the Mountain"

My parents bake Christmas cakes for thirty families on December 23, and we deliver them on Christmas Eve.

—JENNIFER DOWNS, *Newberry*

The Dock Street Theatre

Christmas would not be complete without a performance of Charles Dickens' "A Christmas Carol." An all-new adaptation of this perennial favorite, presented by the Charleston Stage Company in 1996, surely delighted audiences as much as holiday performances first staged at the Dock Street Theatre when it opened in 1736.

Located on the corner of Dock and Church Streets, the original Dock Street Theatre was the first building in America constructed solely for theatrical performances. Historic accounts say that in the 1760s one of the favorite pastimes of John Rutledge, later governor of South Carolina, was to attend the theatre for the purpose of studying history and manners.

There is little record of the fate of the original building, but by the early 1800s the site housed the famed Planter's Hotel, quite possibly the birthplace of the rum concoction known as Planter's Punch. For many years the Planter's Hotel was the principal lodging in Charleston, renowned for its luxury accommodations. One of its most notorious guests was John Wilkes Boothe, the actor who later assassinated Abraham Lincoln. After the Civil War, the hotel fell into ruin.

In the 1930s the Dock Street Theatre was again reborn, this time as an undertaking of the Franklin Roosevelt's Works Progress Administration. Using the shell of the old hotel, architect Alfred Simons modeled the theatre after London period playhouses, featuring beautiful woodwork carved from native cypress trees.

Since 1978, the Charleston Stage Company, directed by Julian Wiles, has performed over 120 productions at the Dock Street Theatre, entertaining more than 35,000 patrons a year. Each December, the ghosts of Christmases past, present, and future take to the stage, teaching Scrooge the meaning of Christmas and delighting audiences with theatrical magic.

Marley's ghost appears at the Dock Street Theatre

The Charleston Stage Company Players

In 1989, sixteen inches of snow fell at Christmas in Seneca. The neighbor kids hardly knew what to do, especially the little ones who were afraid to go out because the snowdrifts were deeper than they were tall.

—SANDRA DERRICK

Ice storm near Walhalla

On December 20, 1989, the weatherman predicted the possibility of a white Christmas, virtually unheard of in Myrtle Beach. By December 24, there was no doubt—it began to flurry, then blizzard. The family arrived to find us knee-deep in snow! What a time we had on the beach, watching the waves break on the snow instead of sand. We had snowball fights and built snowmen, and the neighbors pulled the children along the beach on sleds. It was a winter wonderland and a "new tradition" for us. I wonder if it will ever come again?

—TERRY WILLIAMS, *North Myrtle Beach*

Left: Dawn at Hunting Island State Park
Overleaf: Table Rock State Park and the Greenville Watershed

Holiday Events

Abbeville

Dickens' Village Holiday Open
House, A Taste of Abbeville
Second weekend in November

Christmas Parade and Tour of
Homes, A Taste of Gypsy
First Saturday in December

Aiken

Children's Tree Decorating
Weekend before Thanksgiving

Blessing of the Hounds at
Hitchcock Woods
Thanksgiving Day

Santa Arrives at Aiken Mall/
Carolighting
Friday after Thanksgiving

Fall Steeplechase
Saturday after Thanksgiving

Downtown Merchants' Open House
Sunday after Thanksgiving

Hanukkah, The Festival of Lights
Annual Hanukkah dates

Living Christmas Tree,
Millbrook Baptist Church
Early December

USCA Choir Concerts
First week in December

Christmas by the Lake
First week in December

Christmas Craft Show
First weekend in December

Jaycee Christmas Parade
Second Sunday in December

Choral Society Winter Concerts
Second weekend in December

Family Day Downtown
Second weekend in December

The Holly Spree Craft Fair
Second weekend in December

Choral Society Tour of Homes
Second weekend in December

Holiday Pops Symphony
Performance
Mid-December

Christmas at Hopelands
Third week of December

Kwanzaa Celebration
Late December

First Night Celebration
December 31

Allendale

Annual Holiday Arts and Crafts Fair
Third week in November

Anderson

First Baptist Church
Sanctuary Choir
First week in December

Christmas Gala
First weekend in December

Anderson Girls' Choir Christmas
Concert, Anderson College
Second week in December

Greater Anderson Christmas
Holiday Festival
Mid-December

Bamberg County

Bamberg County Christmas Parade
First Saturday in December

Bamberg County Court House
Carol and Lighting Ceremony
First Sunday in December

Bastesburg-Leesville

Country Christmas Craft Show
First week in December

Beaufort

Tree Lighting
Early December

Christmas Parade
Weekend in early December

Christmas at the Verdier House
Christmas week

Beech Island

Redcliffe Plantation State Park
Christmas Celebration
Second Saturday in December

Berkeley County

Holiday at Nesbit House Drop-In,
Moncks Corner
Early December

Goose Creek Annual Tree Lighting
First week in December

Hanahan Annual Tree Lighting
First weekend in December

Moncks Corner Annual Parade
and Tree Lighting
First Sunday in December

Blacksburg

Christmas Open House,
Kings Mountain State Park
First weekend in December

Brattonsville

Bratton Plantation Candlelight
Christmas Tour
First weekend in December

Camden

Christmas Candlelight
Tour of Homes
Mid-December

Cayce

Christmas Traditions
First week in December

Charleston

Holiday Crafts Fair
November

Annual Lowcountry
Christmas Festival
November

Holiday Festival of Lights
Mid-November to early January

Christmas Aboard the
Charles Towne Princess
Late November through December

Christmas Boat Parade
Early December

Christmas Carriage Tours
December through early January

Plantation Christmas
at Middleton Place
December

Christmas Holiday Walking Tour
December

Serenade at the Charleston
Music Hall
December

Visions of Christmas Past
December

Christmas at Kiawah Island Resort
December

Christmas Lights in
the Lowcountry Tours
December

Christmas at Hampton Plantation
First three weeks in December

Annual Progressive Dinner
in Historic Charleston
Weekends in December

Hollydays in Summerville
Town Square
Weekends in December

Holiday House Tour
First weekend in December

"A Christmas Carol,"
Dock Street Theatre
Second week in December

Annual Dickens' Christmas Show
and Festival
Second weekend in December

Festival of Tablesettings
Second weekend in December

Annual Spirituals Concert
Second weekend in December

Christmas on Mazyck Wragborough
Mid-December

Camellia Christmas at
Magnolia Plantation
Weekends in mid-December

Family Yuletide
Third week in December

Cheraw

Decorating the Town with
Natural Greens
Early December

Cheraw Christmas Parade
Wednesday in early December

Chrismons Tree
December

Cherokee County/Gaffney

College Drive Luminaries
First two weeks in December

Chesterfield

Christmas Time in Olde Chesterfield,
Parade and Tree Lighting
First Thursday in December

Clemson

"The Messiah" Sing-Along,
Clemson University
December

Clinton

Annual Madrigal Dinner and
Concert, Presbyterian College
First weekend in December

Clover

Clover Christmas Tour of Homes
Second Thursday in December

Columbia

Carolina Craftsmen's
Christmas Classic
Mid-November

Columbia Marionette Theatre
Christmas Production
*Mid-November through
early January*

Festival of Trees
Third weekend in November

Vista Lights, Vista Open House
Walking Tour & Performing Arts,
Congaree
Third weekend in November

Jamil Christmas Craft Show
Thanksgiving weekend

"A Christmas Carol," Koger Center
Thanksgiving weekend

Governor's Carolighting
Thanksgiving weekend

Victorian Christmas Faire,
Lexington's Old Mill
*Last weekend in November
through Christmas Eve*

"The Night Before Christmas"
December

"The Nutcracker"
December

Riverbanks Zoo and Garden,
Lights Before Christmas
December

Christmas Open House at the
Governor's Mansion
First week in December

Junior League Holiday Market
First week in December

Cayce Historical Museum Annual
Christmas Traditions
First week in Deceber

Christmas Light Boat Parade,
Lake Murray Dam
First weekend in December

Christmas Tree Lighting with Choir
and Chorus, Columbia College
First weekend in December

Carolina Carillon Holiday Parade
First Saturday in December

Historic Columbia Foundation
Christmas Candlelight Tour of
Homes
Second week in December

First Baptist Church Annual
Columbia Christmas Pageant
Second weekend in December

Shandon Baptist Church,
The Singing Christmas Tree
Second weekend in December

Christmas Sampler Craft Show
at Tri-city Leisure Center
Mid-December

McKissick Museum Children's
Holiday Fest
Mid-December

Palmetto Mastersingers
Christmas Concert
Third week in December

Holiday Pops
Weekend before Christmas

First Night Columbia
December 31

Darlington

Santa's Workshop
Early December

Easley

Annual Christmas Parade
First weekend in December

Festival of Trees
First three weekends in December

Edgefield

Edgefield Tour of Churches
and Christmas Tree Lighting
Early December

Elgin

Catfish Stomp
First weekend in December

Folly Beach

Folly Beach Christmas Fest
December

Fort Mill

Festival of Lights
*Late November through
early January*

Annual Christmas Parade
First Thursday after Thanksgiving

Fountain Inn

Christmas Parade
First Wednesday in December

Spirit of Christmas Past Festival
*First Wednesday in December
(for 12 days)*

Carriage Rides through
Candlelit Streets
Nightly during festival

Live Nativity
Throughout festival

Home Tours
Throughout festival

Breakfast with Santa
Throughout festival

Gaffney/Cherokee County

College Drive Luminaries
First two weeks in December

Georgetown

Festival of Trees
First weekend in December

Christmas Tour of Homes
Second weekend in December

Grand Strand

Treasures by the Sea
November 1 through mid-February

Greenville

"The Nutcracker,"
Carolina Ballet Theatre
Late November

Zoo Lights at Christmas
December

Holiday Lights at Roper Mountain
December

Holiday Fair Arts and Crafts Show
First week in December

University Christmas Oratorio,
Furman University
First weekend in December

Light Up The City,
Tree Lighting Ceremony
First weekend in December

Christmas Tree Lighting and
Caroling, Bob Jones University
First weekend in December

Christmas On Ice
Second week in December

Holiday At Peace Concert,
Greenville Symphony
Second week in December

Annual Holiday Party for Children
Mid-December

Festival of Trees Holiday Events
Last three weeks in December

First Night Greenville
December 31

Hartsville

Turkey Trot, YMCA
Thanksgiving Day

Festival of Lights
Day after Thanksgiving

Christmas Parade
Second Saturday in December

Hilton Head Island

Annual Christmas Arts and
Crafts Festival
Third week in November

Annual Holiday Arts and
Crafts Show (Hilton Resort)
Last week in November

Annual Lights of Christmas
Celebration, Shelter Cove Harbour
Last week in November

"A Christmas Carol,"
Hilton Head Playhouse
December

Christmas Oratorio, Choral Society
Second weekend in December

Breakfast with Santa
Second weekend in December

Bluffton Christmas Parade
Second weekend in December

Annual Christmas Tour of Homes
Mid-December

Santa Paws Photos
Mid-December

Hilton Head Orchestra Traditional
Christmas Concert
Mid-December

Lowcountry Twelve Days of
Christmas (Westin Resort)
Mid-December to Christmas

Christmas Caroling Hayrides
in Sea Pines
December 23 and 24

Christmas Adult and
Junior Golf Round Robins
December 24

Reindeer Classic (Golf Round Robin),
Sea Pines
December 28

New Years Eve Celebration for Kids
December 31

Inman

Christmas at Hollywild
Late November through December

Isle of Palms

Christmas on the Isle of Palms
First three weeks in December

Lake City

Lake City on Parade
Tuesday before Thanksgiving

Poston Corners Christmas Lights
Thanksgiving to Christmas

The Hanging of the Greens at
First Baptist Church
Early December

Festival of Lights Christmas Parade
First or second Friday in December

The Neck Christmas Parade
Christmas Eve

Lake Wylie

Lights on the Lake
*Second or third Saturday
in December*

Leesville (see Batesburg)

Lexington

Lexington Christmas Parade
First weekend in December

Christmas Carol Lighting
First weekend in December

Outdoor Christmas Drama,
Lake Murray Baptist Church
Mid-December

Christmas Sampler
Mid-December

Christmas Peddler
Mid-December

Christmas Peddler Craft Show
at Lexington Leisure Center
Mid-December

Little River

Intracoastal Christmas Regatta
Saturday after Thanksgiving

McConnells

Christmas Candlelight Tour
First weekend in December

McCormick

Annual Christmas Open House
at the Barn
First Saturday in December

Holiday on Main
Second Saturday in December

Mount Pleasant

Holiday Parade
First weekend in December

Old Village Inn Christmas
Mid-December through Christmas

Mullins

Christmas in Mullins
End of November

Holiday Tours of
The Oaks Plantation and Club
December

Myrtle Beach Area

Treasures by the Sea,
A Festival of Lights
November and December

Annual Dickens' Christmas Show
Second weekend in December

**Old 96 District
(see Abbeville, Clinton,
Edgefield and McCormick)**

Pendleton

Christmas Crafts Event
First weekend in December

Best Christmas Pageant Ever
*First and second weekends in
December*

Rock Hill

Old Fashioned Christmas
Craft Festival
First full weekend in November

Salley

Chitlin' Strut
End of November

Seneca

Old Oconee Christmas Celebration
Early November

Simpsonville

Christmas Parade
First Sunday in December

Six Mile

Old Fashioned Christmas
Celebration
Early December

Christmas Parade
First weekend in December

Spartanburg

Historic Houses Christmas Tours,
Walnut Grove Plantation
*Weekends in November
and December*

Toys of Christmas Past Exhibit
*Third weekend of November
through mid-December*

Dickens of a Christmas Festival
Early December

"The Messiah," Wofford College
First weekend in December

"The Nutcracker," Spartanburg
Civic Ballet and Spartanburg
Philharmonic, Converse College
Second weekend in December

Bill Drakes Christmas
Music Festival
Mid-December

New Year's Eve Concert Gala,
Converse College
December 31

Springmaid Beach

Springmaid Beach Annual
Craft Show
First weekend in December

Summerville

Summerville Antique Annual
Open House
Early December

Holly Days: Strolling Carolers
Weekends in December

Christmas Parade on Main Street
Mid-December

Sumter

Fantasy of Lights
December

Singing Christmas Tree
First weekend in December

Holiday House Tour and
Christmas Tea
First Wednesday in December

Candlelight Tour of Homes
Second Saturday in December

Boykin Christmas Parade
Second Sunday in December

Sumter Christmas Parade
First weekend in December

Union

Downtown Merchants' Christmas
Open House
*Late November and
early December*

Open House at Rose Hill Plantation
Early December

Christmas Parade
Second Saturday in December

Walterboro

Holiday Arts Council Concert
Second Sunday in December

Historical and Preservation Society
Tour of Homes
Mid-December

Williamston

Williamston Christmas Park
December

Winnsboro

Dickens' Christmas Show
and Festival
Second weekend in November

Santa Claus Train
Saturday after Thanksgiving

Christmas Home Tour
First week in December

Christmas Candlelight Open House
First week in December

Museum Candlelight Tour
First weekend in December

York

Candlelight Tour
First weekend in December

Christmas in Olde York Church
and House Tour
Second weekend in December

Thank You, South Carolina

Mary Abercrombie
Joe Alexander
Ken Almore
Dennis and Laura Andrews
Diane Armstrong
Mary Augustine
Gary Ault
Mrs. Betty Barnwell
Cheryl Bateman
Mary Wood Beasley
Paul Begley
Kevin Bentley
Maria Bentley
Beth Bilderback
Linda Bishop
Chief Gilbert Blue
Al Boerman
Becky Booth
Carol Ann Bowers
Polly Bowers
Elizabeth Brabbs
Debbie Branch
Miriam Upton Breckenridge
Brenda Brown
Heidi Brown
Margaret Hamilton Brown
Lisa Buckley
Kenny Bulloch
Nancy Bunch
Debbie Busch
Caesars Head State Park
Emory Campbell
Jane Casey
Barbara Chambers
The Charleston Garden Club
The Charleston Museum
Charleston Stage Company
Rebecca Chason
Terry Cherry
The Citadel
Chaplain Charles T. Clanton
Ann L. Clarke
Cindy Clemmer
Coastal Village Press
Thalia J. Coleman
Ernestine Frederick Conner
Robin Copps
Al Corum
Preston and Mary Covington
Rebecca Crawford
Shelley Crawford
Gene Crocker
Joy, Laurel, and John Crosby
Brain Cuthrell
Bill Davis
Charles A. Davis

Joan Davis
Sarah Davis
Susan Davis
Laurie U. deBettencourt
Elizabeth P. deMontmollin
Betty Dent
Sandra Derrick
Chuck Devlin
Jennifer Downs
Drayton Hall Plantation
Dave Dupree
Buddy and Susan Easler
Ann D. Edwards
Elizabeth and Dan Einstein
Pecolia Ellison
Judith Erickson
Doris Fearrington
Geneva B. Finney
Judith Fluck
Donald Fraser
Clare Frist
Elaine Frye
Mrs. T. Loyd Garrett
Virginia Geraty
Mary Giles
Doug Gilmore
Patty Goff
Walter Gould
Tom Gower
Gwen Gramling
Leslie Graves
Dr. Donald Gray
Kathy Gray
Lorrie Griffith
Winona Hair
Lisa Hall
Susan Hall
The Hallelujah Singers
Judy Hamby
Deborah Hardwick
Jimmie E. Harley
Steve and Marianne Harrison
C. Patton Hash
Mittie Hatch
Amy Haymans
Boog Henderson
Craig Henrich
Beth Herron
Karen Hewitt
Mrs. John F. Hooker, Jr.
Hopsewee Plantation
Jacque Hudgens
Daryle Isaacs
Rhett and Betty Jackson
Kathy Jenkins
Cathy Jenkins

Gina Jolly
John Rutledge House Inn
Ann Keeter
Pat Kennedy
Maura, Billy and Emily Kenny
Mr. and Mrs. Terry Ketterman
Melissa Kiefer
Teresa Kleeblatt
Rebecca Knobeloch
Betty Komegary
George W. Koury
Charlotte Kraay
Patricia Kraay
Alleene and Doug Kracht
Jeremy Kracht
Mary Kracht
Alma Lake
Mary Leverett
Meggett Levin
Patsy Lewis
Vicki Loughner
Heather Lowder
Judy L. Lowder
Vangy Mabry
Jan MacDougal
Sammy MacIntosh
Doug MacLean
Betty Malone
Ned and Kim Marshall
Mr. and Mrs. James Maynard
Mr. and Mrs. B. Palmer
   McArthur
Clebe McClary
Tara McClary
Joesph McGill
Judy McNair
Mary Ann Mills
Jodee Mitchell
Dr. Alexander Moore
Elaine Morgan
Judy Mullinax
June Murph
Andy and Betty Newton
Andy Nicolai
Jennifer Ottervik
Kevin Parker
Joan Harrison Pavy
Nell Virginia McMinn Petty
Sara Petty
Cheryl Postlewait
Jennifer Prince
Doris Reaser
The Rhett House Inn
Gretchen Rhinehardt
Riverbanks Zoo
Kay Robertson

Celia Rocks
Roebuck Greenhouses
David Rowan
Chef Bruce A. Sacino
Alex Sanders
Tom Savage
Mary Ruth Schenk
The Senior Lights
Shandon Baptist Church
Susie Shepard
D. Ray Sigmon
Ed Sigmon
Marlena Smalls
Mardi Smith
Tuzy Snyder
Norma Sorgee
The South Carolina
   Philharmonic
Mayme Sowell
Sarah Spruill
Stephanie Steadman
Alice Barron Stewart
Evie Stewart
Eula May Carlisle Stockman
Jim Stockman
Barbara Stone
Dr. Allen Stokes
Andrè Stokes
Barbara and Wayne Sumpter
Elise Talbert
Beth Thomas
Dorothy M. Thompson
Clay, Carol and Caroline
   Timanus
Toogoodoo Christmas Tree Park
Carol Toris
George and Connie Trask
Troy Tuttle
U.S. Amateur Ballroom
   Association, Columbia Chapter
Susan Wall
Douglas Walters
Frances Ward
Tommie Ward
Peggy West
Richard T. Widman
Peter L. Wilkerson
Terry Williams
Ramona Woo
Amy Wood
Lynn and Ed Wood
Helen Yoder
Tony Youmans
Jim Younts

CHAMBERS OF COMMERCE

Greater Abbeville
104 Pickens Street
Abbeville SC 29260
803-459-4600

Aiken
400 Laurens Street, NW
Aiken SC 29801
803-641-1111

Allendale
P.O. Box 517
Allendale SC 29810
803-584-0082

Anderson Area
P.O. Box 1568
Anderson SC 29622
864-226-3454

Bamberg County
Route 3, Box 215A
Bamberg SC 29003
803-245-4427

Barnwell County
P.O. Box 898
Barnwell SC 29812
803-259-7446

Batesburg/Leasville
P.O. Box 349
Batesburg SC 29006
803-532-4339

Greater Beaufort
P.O. Box 910
Beaufort SC 29901
803-524-3163

Berkeley County
P.O. Box 905
Moncks Corner SC 29461
803-761-8238

Calhoun
P.O. Box 444
St. Matthews SC 29135
803-874-3791

Chapin
P.O. Box 577
Chapin SC 29036
803-345-1100

Charleston
P.O. Box 975
Charleston SC 29402
803-853-8000
803-853-0444

Cheraw
221 Market Street
Cheraw SC 29520
803-537-7681

Cherokee County
P.O. Box 1119
Gaffney SC 29342
864-489-5721

Chester County
P.O. Box 489
Chester SC 29706
803-581-4142

Chesterfield
P.O. Box 230
Chesterfield SC 29709
803-623-2343

Clarendon County
P.O. Box 1
Manning SC 29102
803-435-4405

Clemson
P.O. Box 202
Clemson SC 29633
864-654-1200

Clover
P.O. Box 162
Clover SC 29710
803-222-3312

Greater Columbia
P.O. Box 1360
Columbia SC 29202
800-264-4884

Conway Area
P.O. Box 831
Conway SC 29526
803-248-2273

Darlington County
P.O. Box 274
Darlington SC 29532
803-393-2641

Dillon County
P.O. Box 1304
Dillon SC 29536
803-774-8551

Easley
P.O. Box 241
Easley SC 29641
864-859-2693

Edgefield
P.O. Box 23
Johnston SC 29832
803-275-0010

Edisto
P.O. Box 206
Edisto Beach SC 29438
803-869-3867

Fairfield County
P.O. Box 297
Winnsboro SC 29180
803-635-4242

Greater Florence
P.O. Box 948
Florence SC 29503
803-665-0515

Fort Mill
P.O. Box 1357
Fort Mill SC 29715
803-547-5900

Fountain Inn
P.O. Box 568
Fountain Inn SC 29644
864-862-2586

Georgetown County
P.O. Box 1776
Georgetown SC 29442
803-546-8436
800-777-7705

Greater Greenville
P.O. Box 10048
Greenville SC 29603
864-242-1050

Greenwood Area
P.O. Box 980
Greenwood SC 29648
803-223-8431

Greer
P.O. Box 507
Greer SC 29652
864-877-3131

Hampton County
P.O. Box 122
Hampton SC 29924
803-943-3784

Hardeeville
P.O. Box 307
Hardeeville SC 29927
803-784-3606

Hartsville
P.O. Box 578
Hartsville SC 29550
803-332-6401

Hilton Head Island
P.O. Box 5647
Hilton Head Island SC 29938
803-785-3673

Inman
P.O. Box 145
Inman SC 29349
803-472-3654

Irmo
1246 Lake Murray Boulevard
Irmo SC 29063
803-749-9355

Jasper County
P.O. Box 1267
Ridgeland SC 29936
803-726-8126

Kershaw County
P.O. Box 605
Camden SC 29020
803-432-2525

Lake City
P.O. Box 669
Lake City SC 29560
803-394-8611

Lake Wylie
P.O. Box 5233
Lake Wylie SC 29710
803-831-2827

Lancaster County
604 Main Street, Drawer 430
Lancaster SC 29721
803-283-4105

Landrum
P.O. Box 62
Landrum SC 29356
803-457-4246

Laurens County
P.O. Box 248
Laurens SC 29360
803-833-2716

Lee County
P.O. Box 187
Bishopville SC 29010
803-484-5145

Lexington
P.O. Box 44
Lexington SC 29071
803-359-6113

Greater Liberty
P.O. Box 123
Liberty SC 29657
803-843-1162

Little River
P.O. Box 400
Little River SC 29566
803-249-6604

Loris
P.O. Box 356
Loris SC 29569
803-756-6030

Marion
P.O. Box 35
Marion SC 29571
803-423-3561

Marlboro County
P.O. Box 458
Bennettsville SC 29512
803-479-3941

Mauldin Area
P.O. Box 645
Mauldin SC 29662
864-297-1323

McCormick County
P.O. Box 938
McCormick SC 29835
803-465-2835

Mid-Carolina
Drawer 660
Prosperity SC 29127
803-364-4222

Midland Valley
P.O. Box 305
Clearwater SC 29822
803-593-3030

Greater Mullins
P.O. Box 595
Mullins SC 29574
803-464-6651

Myrtle Beach
P.O. Box 2115
Myrtle Beach SC 29578
803-626-7444

Newberry
P.O. Box 396
Newberry SC 29108
803-276-4274

Ninety Six
P.O. Box 8
Ninety Six SC 29666
803-543-2900

North Augusta
235 Georgia Avenue
North Augusta SC 29841
803-279-2323

North Myrtle Beach
P.O. Box 754
North Myrtle Beach SC 29582
803-249-3519

Orangeburg County
P.O. Box 328
Orangeburg SC 29116
803-534-6821

Pageland
P.O. Box 56
Pageland SC 29728
803-672-6400

Pickens
P.O. Box 153
Pickens SC 29671
864-878-3258

Rock Hill Area
P.O. Box 590
Rock Hill SC 29731
803-324-7500

Saluda County
Law Range
Saluda SC 29138
864-445-3055

Seneca
P.O. Box 855
Seneca SC 29679
864-882-2097

Simpsonville
P.O. Box 605
Simpsonville SC 29681
864-963-3781

South Strand
P.O. Box 650
Murrells Inlet SC 29576
803-651-1010

Spartanburg Area
P.O. Box 1636
Spartanburg SC 29304
864-594-5000

Greater Summerville
P.O. Box 670
Summerville SC 29484
803-873-2931

Greater Sumter
P.O. Box 1229
Sumter SC 29151
803-775-1231

Tega Cay
Four Tega Cay Drive
Tega Cay SC 29715
803-548-2444

Tri-County
P.O. Box 175
Harleyville SC 29448
803-496-3561

Union County
P.O. Box 368
Union SC 29379
864-427-9039

Greater Walhalla Area
220 E. Main Street
Walhalla SC 29691
864-638-2727

Walterboro-Colleton
P.O. Box 426
Walterboro SC 29488
803-549-9595

West Metro
1006 12th Street
Cayce SC 29033
803-794-6504

Westminster
P.O. Box 155
Westminster SC 29693
864-647-5316

Greater Williamsburg
P.O. Box 696
Kingstree SC 29556
803-354-6431

Woodruff
P.O. Box 522
Woodruff SC 29388
864-476-8807

York County
P.O. Box 11377
Rock Hill SC 29731
800-866-5200
805-329-5200

A SOUTH CAROLINA TASTE TEST

On a pleasant April day in 1997, nearly a hundred people from Columbia and nine other South Carolina cities gathered at The Happy Bookseller in Columbia to participate in a taste test for recipes submitted for this book. Organizers Rhett and Betty Jackson, Alleene Kracht, and Ann Keeter made all the arrangements for the dishes to be prepared. Two large tables in the bookstore and one table next door at Lillian's Delicacies were piled with food, which the taste testers then rated. Everyone agreed it was a great success, and the top-rated recipes are published here in *A South Carolina Christmas*. If you're wondering which recipes ranked highest, there was a tie between the Shrimp and Grits and the She-Crab Soup. Close behind were Coconut Cake, Peanut Butter Balls, Butternut Squash, and Sour Cream Pound Cake. We wish to extend a special thanks to all the wonderful organizers, cooks, and tasters!

The Cooks and Bakers

Mary Ellen Adams, Susan Barron, Mosi Bayo, Marjorie Campbell, Shannon L. Carter, Sara Cook, Alberta Dubisz, Bob Ellis, Cris Fox, Marguerite Fox, Andy Graves, Virginia Haney, Betty Jackson, Ann Keeter, Hazel Knowlton, Charlotte Kraay, Alleene and Doug Kracht, Lillian Lippard, Ruth Long, Alice Lucas, Peggy Lynch, Boby Miller, Dorris Motley, Charlotte Myers, Christine Oswold, Sara Petty, Neva Poole, Doris Price, Lola Prough, Brandi Rogerson, Rosina Stephenson, Carrie Stepp, Marcia Watkins, Elizabeth Workman, and Lillian Zografov.

The Tasters

Mary Ellen Adams, Laura and Andrew Arthur, Tim Balei, Bill Barber, Mosi Bayo, Judy Bistany, Denise Bradley, Linda Bradley, David and Miranda Brand, Laney Brant, Abigail R. Brown, Annelore Butler, Marjorie and John Campbell, Frances Goodwin Capps, Shannon Carter, Dorothy Cedar, Randall M. Chastain, Rachel O. Clary, Sara Cook, Jenni Craft, B.J. DeBell, Franklin W. Draper, Alberta and Edwin Dubisz, Dot Duncan, Bob Ellis, Dr. Daniel Feldman, Pat T. Flora, Nell Fowler, Clare Frist, Larry K. and Hume Laub Fulmer, Connie Green, Dan Haltiwanger, Virginia and Paul Haney, Tim Harris, Diane Harrison, Kaaren Hayes, Patricia Hearron, O'Neal Humphries, Betty and Rhett Jackson, Alfred Jayne, Randy and Anna Jones, W. R. Keane, Bronwyn Kemper, Hazel and David Knowlton, Charlotte Kraay, Alleene and Doug Kracht, Jeremy Kracht, Mary Kracht, Mary Lamson, Judith P. Langston, Susan Leach, Jane Lieberman, Shelley Logan, Ruth and Burt Long, Alice and James Lucas, King McLeod, Charlotte and Stanley Meyers, Boby and Harold Miller, Dorris Motley, Christine Oswold, Amy Pearce, Christie Phelps, Cathy H. and Paul A. Pickens, Neva Poole, Doris and John Price, Jenny Prince, Lola and Leo Prough, Ellen Reynolds, Kathryn Richardson, Alana and Meredith Ritchie, Norma Ritchie, Brandi Rogerson, Georgette Sandifer, Minerva W. Sanner, Bob Schlagal, Mary Anne Smith, Michael D. Smith, Carrie Stepp, Lindsey Stevenson, Justin Street, Elizabeth Hope Thomas, James R. Tompkins, Lee Tsiantis, Debbie Turner, Virginia B. Vaughan, JoAnn C., Claude, Jr. and Dorothy Walker, Marcia Watkins, Lee White, Shannon Whitlaw, Melissa Whittaker, Fran Williams, Tracey Elizabeth Williams, and Jim Wilson.

PHOTO CREDITS